YOU WON'T BELIEVE IT

(BUT IT'S TRUE)

YOU WON'T BELIEVE IT

(BUT IT'S TRUE)

One family's journey into
a rare genetic disease.

Dr. Kolleda,

Thank you so much for all
the amazing care you + the
entire staff gave our dear
Birdie ♡

Donna

DONNA A. MARTIN

Design by Jen Bradstreet

ISBN 9780578 273082

Printed in the United States

BRAD

You are my hero.
You were so much more than your illness.
However, you faced your disease with dignity, grace,
and appreciation for all who cared for you.
You never once complained.
You are deeply missed and forever loved.

BRUCE

This is not a journey that any parent should
have to travel, but I know I could not have
trudged through it without you.

GARRETT

You are the best brother ever.

CYNDEE

You loved Brad like no other.

BRAD'S FRIENDS

You know who you are, are all amazing.
Brad was a wealthy man having
each of you as his friend.

CONTENTS

Being one in a million, being rare,
being unique is not always a great thing.

If you have ever heard about a mother's "intuition" and didn't believe it to be true, this story may change your mind. As a mother of two, these accounts of our children's lives and diagnoses are too rare and unusual to be fiction. I'm just not that creative a writer. Frankly, I'm not an author at all and writing a book has never been on my radar or my bucket list. I'm just a mom who needs to tell her story for herself, and maybe for some other parent who has a "sinking" feeling that something isn't right. I want to give that parent encouragement to keep seeking out answers. To keep fighting the fight. To become the advocate that only a parent can be for their child, regardless of that child's age. To not be afraid of the medical community — they don't know everything, and in their defense, they can't do what they don't know. To become a teacher for their doctors, so that their doctors can best treat their child. It's exhausting, but it must be done. It can be done.

What alternative is there?

CHAPTER 1

Pieces of a Mysterious Health Puzzle

From the day Brad was born, something wasn't right. I just knew it. First of all, his chin was severely pushed in, which seemed odd, but with such a difficult delivery we thought it was from the birthing process. Also, he hated to be held. The more you held him, the more he squirmed. The pushed in chin turned out to be the first clue no one picked up on.

My pregnancy was great, though. I never had morning sickness, gained lots of weight, and thoroughly enjoyed the process. At one point my doctor thought Brad was twins, but that wasn't the case.

Delivery was a different story. Being your first, you have no idea what to expect. I have a high pain threshold, and I wasn't dilating so they administered Pitocin. I went from three to ten centimeters in a few short hours, with no pain meds. It was brutal. I was digging my nail into my husband Bruce's back.

"Aah, she's not in pain, she hasn't gone through transition yet," the nurse said at the time.

I missed having a C-section by four minutes. There was a lot of tearing. When it was all over, she apologized to me, saying that she had never seen anyone go through what I went through without saying one word.

Brad's body temperature was very low, and he had trouble breathing. He also had passed some stool into the amniotic fluid, something known as terminal meconium, but they eventually got him to safe levels.

I had post-delivery complications, too. I hemorrhaged severely, and they put me back on Pitocin. Having already had a terrible time with my IV earlier, it took them five tries, even scraping the needle on my bones, before successfully reinserting it. I was freaking out, but eventually Brad and I were both okay and we were released three days later.

Back home, Brad was always in constant motion. The simple task of changing his diapers was almost impossible. I would have to put him on the floor, place one leg over his stomach, and quickly remove, clean, and replace his diaper. My sister-in-law said that she would never have a second child if her first was like Brad.

Everything seemed to happen differently for Brad. He walked at seven months old, completely skipping the crawling stage. Our pediatrician even asked if I wanted two bricks, one for each foot to anchor him down.

Sleeping was never a problem for Brad — or for his brother Garrett, who was born about three-and-a half-years later. They both were "blanket" babies and slept 12 hours every night. And, as if that wasn't enough sleep, Garrett used to take five-hour naps from 10 a.m. to 3 p.m. *Yes!* The first time he did it, thinking the worst, I put a mirror under his nose to see if he was breathing!

By nine months, Brad was running around. He always liked to be in motion, but didn't talk until he was almost three-and-a-half years old, which also seemed odd. Bruce used to travel extensively. Typically, he was only home for about 48 hours a week, so at first it was just Brad and me, and we developed our own form of communication. Other parents couldn't believe I was able to figure out whatever he "grunted," but we managed.

By age six, I started seeing spots of blood in Brad's underpants while doing laundry. This couldn't be normal and I was concerned. Our pediatrician recommended a urologist. We learned that Brad had a urethral stricture that had to be addressed. The stricture was preventing him from voiding completely, doubling the size of one of his kidneys. He needed a urethral dilation.

This is an outpatient procedure, and Bruce and I were able to be in the procedure room with Brad. It was 1992, and the doctor, whose name I don't recall, decided to use local anesthesia instead of general anesthesia. Someone trying to put something into his private parts was unbearable for a little six-year-old boy. He flipped out. Bruce flipped out. The doctor walked out. He called our pediatrician immediately and told her he refused to ever operate on our son again if my husband was there. We found a different doctor.

This was the first of nine or ten strictures. We lost count. During one of Brad's dilations he had a severe reaction to an anesthetic called Versed. He was seven or eight at the time and began hallucinating. It took two of us to keep him from leaping off the gurney to "capture the balloons and dinosaurs."

Once we understood the stricture process, everything seemed relatively okay. But there were other small things that were odd: he started to go gray when he was eleven. *Hmmm?* By fourteen, his fingernails and toenails looked terrible. I don't mean just not pretty, I mean terrible. It seemed like there was some kind of deficiency in all 20 nails. A dermatologist we visited said he had 20 nail dysplasia, but it wasn't anything serious. He was just going to have ugly nails. *Hmmm?* At the time we didn't know that these were all pieces of a puzzle that would come together later to reveal a devastating picture.

Just before Brad's 18th birthday, he had another stricture recurrence, and a wound on his hand that wouldn't heal that he had gotten while volunteering for the Yarmouth Fire Department. He went back to his pediatrician, who decided to do a routine complete blood count, called a CBC.

CHAPTER 2

Everything was normal on Monday.
On Tuesday, our family's life changed forever.

It was Tuesday. Our doctor called to say we needed to get Brad to
Maine Medical Center the next day for a bone marrow aspiration!
What!? What were they talking about? Because Brad was not quite
18 yet, our pediatrician connected us with Dr. Eric Larsen of the
Maine Children's Cancer Program (MCCP), in Scarborough, Maine.
Cancer Program! What the hell was going on? Dr. Larsen met us
at Maine Medical Center in Portland on Wednesday morning and
talked us through our first aspiration. Our heads were spinning.
This had come out of nowhere. We didn't even really understand
why Brad needed it. We were told his CBCs were low; his bilirubin
was high. This was completely cryptic to us at the time. What did
it all mean?

While Brad was prepped for surgery, they told us they would plunge
a very large syringe into Brad's rear pelvic region and draw out a
sample of bone marrow. The results would come in three stages: a
current CBC on the same day, a second reading of the sample in
24 hours, and final results in two weeks.

After we received the first results that Wednesday, Dr. Larsen and
a woman — I think her name was Nancy — who was an MCCP
social worker sat down with me while Brad was in recovery. They

put their arms around me and had "that" look — the knowing look that meant they were getting ready to deliver bad news. Brad had bone marrow failure. We would not know how severe it was, or to what degree, until we got the final results in two weeks later.

When monitoring a patient with bone marrow failure, several levels within the blood are examined:

- White Blood Counts (WBC) – Normal Range: 4.2–9.9

- Hemoglobin (HGB) – Normal Range: 13–17

- Hematocrit (HCT) – Normal Range: 30s–40s

- Platelets – Normal Range: 140–440

- Absolute Neutrophil Count (ANC) – Normal Range: 1500+

- Red Blood Count (RBC) – Normal Range: 4.5–5.9

- Mean Corpuscular Volume (MCV) – Normal Range: 80–96

Each of these parts of the blood has a purpose, and they all have a range of where they should be. If a value is too high or too low, it's a flag for a health issue.

WBCs help fight infection. The ANC represents the ratio of which white blood cells can fight infection. Again, a range is critical. For ANCs, higher values are always better. However, as the numbers get lower with bone marrow failure, the lower the ANC number, the higher the risk for infection. When this number hits 500 or lower, a patient is at very high risk for infection and may even be quarantined.

Platelets are necessary for the blood to be able to clot, which is important so a person doesn't bleed or bruise easily or excessively.

MCVs measure the size of a patient's blood cells. There is a school of thought that there might be a connection between larger MCVs and the progression of bone marrow failure.

One of the ways to measure bone marrow failure is called its "cellularity" level. The lower the cellularity percentage, the more advanced the failure.

All this is, of course, only rudimentary information about the amazing things our blood does every day. Not being a doctor, a hematologist, or an oncologist, I don't have enough information to elaborate much more. I can only give you the limited knowledge I have, in the simplest way I can to explain our story.

Those two weeks of waiting for the final results were hell. We finally got the them. They showed that Brad currently did not have leukemia, but his cellularity level was only about 20%. Dr. Larsen was stumped. There was no evidence of any cancers, but the bone marrow failure was definitely there.

One thing that Dr. Larsen emphasized was that we should stay off the internet about this. This was 2005, and although the internet had come a long way in terms of reliable medical information and diagnosing of illnesses, it was still far from being reliably accurate. Even today, it is a tool that should be used carefully. We were in shock at the time, so we did exactly as we were told.

Over the next year and a half, Brad had several bone marrow aspirations, all with relatively the same results. Bruce and I would hold our breath until results came in. I would cry for two weeks waiting for them. We were fumbling in the dark. When the results arrived, we would cry if they went down or exhale if they went slightly up. It was a roller coaster ride and we had no idea where the track was. At that time, we didn't really understand what the results meant.

Finally, after a year and a half, I went on the previously forsaken internet. I couldn't take it anymore — I needed more information. One thing I've learned about myself throughout this journey is that I'm a researcher by nature. I need information, data, supporting material. It's the way I address everything. I don't make a large purchase of anything without making my own form of a spread sheet. I weigh pros and cons. I accept facts. Speculation is a waste of time.

Poking around on the internet, plugging in bone marrow failure tens of different ways, I stumbled onto something that startled me and made me keep digging. I found a list of many types of diseases that were associated with bone marrow failure. This list is quite long, but anyone can go to the Aplastic Anemia and Myelodysplastic Syndrome Foundation (https://www.aamds.org) and review the many diseases.

I started opening the links to each disease and reading each of the traits associated with it. None fit. Brad didn't have any of them. I opened the link for a disease called Dyskeratosis Congenita (DC), pronounced *Dis - Ker - a -Tos - is Con - Jen - i - Ta*. What the hell was this? I couldn't even pronounce it. I kept scrolling through all its traits and almost fell off my desk chair when I saw "20 Nail Dysplasia." My heart stopped. I kept reading, but in late 2006 there wasn't very much information about this disease online.

The next time we spoke with Dr. Larsen, we mentioned it right away, but he really didn't believe it could be Dyskeratosis Congenita. He had been discussing Brad's idiopathic bone marrow failure with colleagues from around the country. (Idiopathic just means that no one knows what is causing a disease.) He continued to bring up Brad's case for years, and Brad continued to have bone marrow aspirations — eight aspirations in seven years.

YOU WON'T BELIEVE IT (BUT IT'S TRUE)

CHAPTER 3

Game Changer —
On a Small Piece of Paper

By now it was October 2011, and I ran into a friend whose husband was dying of non-Hodgkin's lymphoma. She mentioned his WBC and ANC and a drug that he was given to help improve those numbers. He was a patient at the Dana Farber Cancer Institute (DFCI) in Boston, Massachusetts. Again, my heart sank, and a bell went off. It was such a random conversation, but I felt with all my being that we needed to go to DFCI. Maybe they could help Brad. Maybe they could give him the same drug to help his WBC. I asked to have Brad referred there.

For the record, Dr. Larsen has always been great to us. From day one, he always let us know that if we wanted a second opinion, he would support it. Because we saw him at the hospital, Brad wasn't technically his patient, but he continued to try to get to the bottom of Brad's case for over seven years. Dr. Larsen would always take our calls, and even would follow up with us while on vacation. He is an exceptional person.

Bruce, Brad, and I went to DFCI in late November 2011. We met Dr. Eva Guinan and her assistant Lisa Brennan. After talking for a while, Brad was thoroughly examined and blood was taken. His follow up was on December 8, 2011. Brad and I went back to Boston to meet with Eva and Lisa again. The four of us were in a small room.

"Before we begin, does anyone have any questions?" Eva said, as we got settled in.

"Yes!" I said, as I jumped up and got out the folder that I had been keeping on Brad, including all of his CBC results and any other information I had regarding his case.

"I have this name of a disease on a small piece of paper that's been in Brad's file for five and a half years. I can't pronounce it. I was hoping we could test for it and, if nothing else, rule it out."

I handed them the piece of paper. The note read: Dyskeratosis Congenita. The room went silent. Eva and Lisa looked at each other, stunned, not unlike the way Dr. Larsen and Nancy had looked at me seven years earlier.

"That is exactly what Brad has — Dyskeratosis Congenita," Eva said.

I was angry — not at Dr. Larsen, not at anyone, but at the fact that I had been asking repeatedly, for over five and a half years, if we could test for this. I could never let it go. Also, it made me so mad that a mom could find this rare disease by matching one trait on the internet.

Here's a short description of what Dyskeratosis Congenita is. It's a brief overview, but a devastating snapshot.

- Less than one in a million people are diagnosed with it.

- Less than 500 people worldwide have been diagnosed to date.

- Males are diagnosed 3 to 1.

- Most patients succumb to bone marrow failure and/or pulmonary fibrosis.

- Most patients are at very high risk for many cancers and leukemias.

- Most patients don't survive past 16 and, on the outside, 30 years of age.

Most importantly, Dyskeratosis Congenita is a telomere biology disorder. I'll discuss this key fact in more detail later in our story.

Eva explained the basic triad of symptoms that most DC patients had, and Brad had all three:

- Reticular hyper-pigmentation (a lacey patterning on the skin of the upper torso, neck, and head.)

- Oral Leukoplakia (white precancerous patches in the mouth)

- 20 Nail Dysplasia *(!!!)*

Since my initial internet search, much more has been discovered and written about Dyskeratosis Congenita. We now know that Brad has 16 DC traits.

So, what is Dyskeratosis Congenita? It is a rare genetic disease. It's not an autoimmune disease, which is what the Maine Children's Cancer Program had been looking for, and why Brad's went undiagnosed. Dyskeratosis Congenita is so rare that most of the medical community is not even aware of it. Until recently, there haven't even been any clinical guidelines for Dyskeratosis Congenita.

Beginning with that meeting, Eva started scheduling tests to get a baseline for Brad's Dyskeratosis Congenita. She also introduced us to Dr. Suneet Agarwal from Boston Children's Hospital. Suneet was conducting a genetic bone marrow study, and asked if Brad would be part of it.

Brad had agreed to be part of the study. When Suneet left the room to get what was necessary for his participation, we had a brief moment alone. What Brad said next floored me: "Mom, the reason I am choosing to be part of this study is because even though I may not live to benefit from it, someone else will."

It was all happening too fast. This was surreal. My heart was breaking for Brad at that appointment.

He was being given a death sentence at 25. We were being told we might not have him with us much longer.

Before we left Boston that day, Eva told us her main current concern about Brad was that his platelets were low, around 50. She was worried that if Brad got into a car accident and had a head injury, he could bleed internally.

On December 31, early New Year's Eve morning, that is exactly what happened.

Driving on an icy road, Brad hit an embankment, went airborne, and hit a tree. The car flipped heel over toe five or six times into the woods by a quiet road. When the police found the car, they said not only that was Brad lucky to be alive, but that he should have died from the extent of the accident. Five people in Maine died on icy roads from the ice storm that day. Brad should have been number six.

Bruce and I woke to the phone ringing that morning. It was Brad on the other end, telling us he had been in a car accident and was at the Yarmouth Fire Department, where he had volunteered since he was 16. He was very committed and passionate about his service to the department. Going there must have been a comforting place for him. Except he wasn't making sense on the phone, and then he hung up. We were concerned and confused. We got out of bed and called the fire department. They told us that he was bleeding, badly bruised, and was being transported to Maine Medical Center (MMC).

We began to freak out. I called MMC several times and asked to be connected to the Emergency Department. We kept being disconnected. I couldn't breathe and started having a panic attack. My only thought was that Brad had internal bleeding and no one would know to check for this. He was not a normal accident patient — he had Dyskeratosis Congenita! Bruce suggested we contact Dr. Larsen, who was still part of Brad's medical team at that time. We called Maine Children's Cancer Program. It was a Saturday, so of course it went to the answering service. We described the urgency of Brad's situation and asked to have Dr. Larsen call us. He called right away.

It's odd how some things work out sometimes. Dr. Larsen was on call at MMC and in the hospital when he called us! He rushed over to the ER immediately and explained Brad's medical situation so he could be evaluated accurately. Nothing is easy for DC patients. Everything is extreme, hard, intense, and rare.

To make matters worse, Bruce and I were over 130 miles away, at our place in Sugarloaf for the Christmas and New Year holidays. The house was still completely decorated for Christmas and our friends Dianne and Michael were staying with us. My anxiety attack got worse. By now I had been on the floor struggling to breathe for 45 minutes. Bruce thought I might be having a heart attack.

Dianne and Michael stepped up to the plate in a huge way. Michael took care of our two dogs. Dianne helped Bruce rip down all the decorations, pack them, and store them in two hours flat! It usually takes a couple of days to accomplish this. Now all we had to do was get down the mountain in an ice storm.

When I finally picked Brad up at the hospital, l burst into tears and was almost sick. He looked awful, and so bruised, but he was able to walk out of the hospital. I think something was in a sling, I can't remember. I don't think I'll ever get over that image. He was on bed rest for a while and wouldn't drive for over a month after being so shaken up.

It turned out that when Brad "came to" after the accident, in a field, he somehow managed to walk to the main road sometime before 6 a.m. An amazing good Samaritan saw him and brought him to the fire department. We never knew this person's name and have never been able to thank her or him. We are grateful to this person to this day.

Brad didn't remember the accident and wouldn't look at pictures of the car, which for some reason I can't seem to erase from my phone. It is an ever-present reminder of how lucky we were to still have him after an accident that should have taken him from us.

Shortly afterwards, Brad was scheduled for his first Pulmonary Function Test (PFT). This test measures the capacity and health of the lungs. Brad was still badly bruised and sore from the accident. He was miserable, but he was undergoing more testing. It was a gray day. The halls at MMC were an unwelcoming, cold, fluorescent white. I remember sitting in the waiting room, tucked in the corner, while they escorted Brad behind the door for still another test. We learned the results of those tests results later that month, in January 2012. Brad had Pulmonary Fibrosis, along with his Dyskeratosis Congenita and bone marrow failure. How could this be?

YOU WON'T BELIEVE IT (BUT IT'S TRUE)

CHAPTER 4

New Reality —
I Had the Handouts to Prove It

All this reality was becoming too much for me. I started to shut
down. One day at Sugarloaf all by myself, I cried for almost 24
hours. I was spent. I woke up Saturday morning with such a heavy
heart. I could physically feel it pulling me down. I had a bloody
Mary. I took a nap. Woke up and had a glass of wine. Took another
nap. I was crying so hard I was sobbing. It was a sob I had never
heard come out of my body. It rose from my toes. It wiped me out.
I kept saying "why?" — and texting Bruce, because I literally couldn't
speak. I can't remember if I ate anything at all. It was the seven years
of not knowing, seven years of a pall over us, and then the reality of
the diagnosis. I was mourning the loss of what most likely might
never be. No parent should have to know the pain of possibly losing
a child, and this was, is, now Bruce's and my reality. Why?

That day at Sugarloaf was in March 2012. The next day I got back
on the internet and started to seek out as much additional
information on Dyskeratosis Congenita as I could. I learned that
Dr. Inderjeet Dokal of London is credited for discovering the
genetic basis of the disease. In the early days, it was called Zinsser-
Engman-Cole Syndrome. I learned about the research being done,
along with any pieces of other information I could find about it.
Then something amazing happened.

I found a link to a nonprofit just for Dyskeratosis Congenita! I couldn't believe my eyes. This was surreal! There was a whole group of DC patients out there communicating through this site, Dyskeratosis Congenita Outreach (DCO), now called Team Telomere (https:// teamtelomere.org). I opened every page and link on the site. I think I was in shock. Scouring the website, I learned of a retreat that was being held at Camp Sunshine in Casco, Maine in October 2012! Could this be true? Casco, Maine is in my back yard! How could I attend? I immediately contacted then president and cofounder of DCO, Nancy Cornelius. She was a DC patient herself and an amazing advocate for seeking knowledge about Dyskeratosis Congenita, not only for herself and her son, who was also a DC patient, but for DC patients all around the world.

To my surprise, Nancy responded to my email immediately. After a few more emails, we spoke on the phone.

So many aspects of this disease have been life-changing for our family. My connection to Nancy was no different. I was speaking to another human being who knew about Dyskeratosis Congenita. Up until that point I felt like an alien. She welcomed me into the DC "family" immediately! She gave me so much new information about Dyskeratosis Congenita that my head was swimming. She strongly encouraged me to attend Camp and walked me through the application process.

The time between my conversation with Nancy and the retreat seemed to drag on for what felt like forever. I was very anxious, but I knew I had to attend. My family wasn't ready to go and I understood. It had only been 10 months since we received all this shocking news.

Camp was an entirely new piece of DC baggage that most of us weren't ready wrap our brains around. Nothing was going to stop me from going, however. Since I was attending by myself and I live in Maine, I was not comfortable sleeping on campus. It didn't seem right to take up a bed and funding if I lived so close. (Families from around the world attend Camp for free, so available funds are precious.)

Carol, a dear friend's mother-in-law and her husband John let me stay at their year-round house on Thompson Lake in Poland, Maine, which is about 20 minutes from Casco. I didn't know it at the time, but being able to leave the campus and have the solace of the lake at the end of the day was a great gift.

October 10, 2012, the first day of the retreat had arrived. The retreat ran from Wednesday through Sunday. Wednesday was for welcoming all the families, getting them registered, and checking in. Even though I live in Maine and had heard about Camp Sunshine for years, I had never been to the campus. As a family we had supported Camp Sunshine in various ways before, but now it was entirely different. We were now a Camp Sunshine family.

I felt like I was walking through wet cement just trying to get through the door. I took a deep breath. I was very scared for some reason. Again, I had felt like an alien. Then something amazing happened. I met Nancy Cornelius for the first time in person. She greeted me with a huge smile and even bigger hug. Nancy introduced me to Nancy Cincotta, who is the Camp's Psychosocial Director. This Nancy also greeted me with a huge hug and smile, and then said something that really took me by surprise.

33

"I'm so glad you're here, and this is going to sound weird, but you are our only DC family from Maine!"

"Yes, it is weird, but I get it," I said.

Brad's brother Garrett, who can always make me laugh, even at the darkest times and in the sweetest way, put it best:

"So, Mom, let me see if I understand this. DC is diagnosed less than one in a million, right? Maine's population is 1.3 million, so Brad's it?"

Again, being so rare is not always so great.

I got to the lake Wednesday night, the first of my three nights there. It became a kind of home for me — a huge warm blanket that enveloped me. Carol and John were so kind to let me stay there and let me sleep in their master bedroom. Every morning I woke to see the mist that hovered over the lake. It was a beautiful way to start a day, especially knowing Camp sessions were going to be tough.

Camp started at 9 a.m. sharp. I was sure to be there early because I didn't want to miss a moment. The sessions were long and intense. Experts from around the world were there — in rustic Casco, Maine — there because of this rare genetic disease that was directly affecting my family, the only family in Maine known to be diagnosed with Dyskeratosis Congenita. My head was being crammed non-stop with new knowledge about it.

I was stunned to see so many families with Dyskeratosis Congenita. They came from all over — from New Zealand, Australia, Canada, Ireland — and from across the United States. Suddenly something hit me — we were all aliens, only now we were all speaking the same language. It was amazing, but since Brad's diagnosis, my family had been in this little dark bubble with no one to talk to about Dyskeratosis Congenita, and now I was in a huge lecture hall filled with families that were affected by Dyskeratosis Congenita. We were not alone anymore. We had a new family, our Camp Sunshine family.

Each day at Camp, Nancy Cincotta led a parent group session in an open dialogue about what they were going through. The session typically started with the parents introducing themselves. From there the conversation could go in many directions. Since I was new to the group, it was my turn to tell our story. After I did, one gentleman, Paul from New Zealand, stood up, crossed over the circle, and gave me a big hug. He was crying. I was stunned. This man was crying for me and he had two sons with Dyskeratosis Congenita and had lost his eldest not very long ago. It felt almost wrong to accept the hug, but it would have also been very wrong not to. This was my new Camp family. They had welcomed me into this unusual tribe.

This was the second retreat DCO offered. The first was in 2010, so some of the families at Camp Sunshine already knew each other. More and more families have attended subsequent retreats, which means that more DC cases are being diagnosed, and also that the medical community as a whole is slowly becoming more aware of the disease. But with every new retreat, there are also more people we have lost. Those families don't come back. DCO moves mountains for its patients, families, and even the medical community.

Every day at Camp left me speechless and practically lifeless. I would stop at a local market, pick up something for dinner and plop down as soon as I got back to the lake. There was a television at the lake house, but for some reason I wasn't able to get it to work, which is no surprise because I am electronically challenged. It's not that I can't learn, I just don't care enough to learn. I would watch movies on my laptop until I couldn't keep my eyes open and would crash into bed each night.

After three long, intense, information-saturated days, I headed for home. I called Bruce and told him I was too tired to cook, too spent to go out, and didn't want to see anyone besides him. I had to purge all I had experienced. I bought a pizza and wine, got home, and wept. I cried and cried. I was mentally exhausted. This new DC reality was almost unbearable. As I shared my experience, Bruce began to cry, too. That night I was sobbing in my sleep, and Bruce had to keep comforting me. The reality of this horrible disease was now laid out before our eyes — I had the handouts to prove it. My brain was on overload from all this new information and I wasn't quite sure what to do with it.

After Camp, I felt compelled to share my experience with family and friends in a one-page letter.

We asked Brad if he was okay if we did this. An amazing thing about Brad was that he was always a black and white, factual person. The reason he agreed to be part of Suneet's genetic bone marrow study was that, even though he knew the reality of his diagnosis, he also genuinely cared about people and felt if being part of the study — or writing my letter — would help raise awareness and understanding of Dyskeratosis Congenita, he was for it. It was never in Brad's comfort zone to have attention focused on himself. It was his passion for the wellbeing of other people that drew him to the fire department, for instance. Since we hadn't really gone public with Dyskeratosis Congenita up to this point, the letter would be brief to spare people, but would also ask them to support our small, off the radar, nonprofit and/or Camp Sunshine, which had both become so valuable to our family.

Networking from Camp has proven to be an unbelievable asset. There is no price that can be attached to how much it means to meet the families, the board members, and the medical advisory committee at Camp. And — this can't be said enough — families pay nothing to attend. Each family gets the opportunity to have private "one-on-ones" with any or all the doctors who attend. For families dealing with such a dire diagnosis, those opportunities are truly priceless. All the doctors are engaged and approachable. They listen. They are patient. They are generous. Where else can you meet with a world class doctor — in any field — and be able to sit in a casual atmosphere, ask all your questions, and have the doctor genuinely interested in what you have to say?

Our medical advisory board doctors know that, as DC families, many of us know more about the disease than a lot of our doctors at home. We are the educators and advocates. We approach every doctor's appointment armed with the latest DC information to be certain they are aware of it. The great challenge for the medical community is that Dyskeratosis Congenita has so many variants, and no two patients are alike, often not even within the same family. Our Camp doctors are aware of this and are thrilled to have so many DC families attend, giving them an opportunity to learn from us, as well!

CHAPTER 5

National Institutes of Health (NIH) — Just Under the Wire

Drs. Blanche Alter and Sharon Savage both encouraged Brad to consider becoming part of the National Institutes of Health's Bone Marrow Failure Study. We talked with Brad to see if this was something he would be willing to do. It was a tremendous commitment. It required flying to Bethesda, Maryland, staying in a hotel for a week, and committing to participating in whatever tests and procedures they requested. As a participant, it is always your choice to not endure certain tests or procedures, but the NIH greatly hopes that you do.

Brad agreed to go to Maryland. His reasoning was twofold. First, he knew it would help increase understanding of Dyskeratosis Congenita. But also, just as important, he was now almost two years into his diagnosis (not including the seven years before we had a diagnosis). He was tired of being poked and prodded, and who could blame him? He had endured eight bone marrow aspirations, countless CBCs, and — since his diagnosis — pulmonary tests, trips to the dermatologist, to an ophthalmologist, and twice-yearly visits to an ear, nose, and throat specialist to have a scope put down his throat to check for oral leukoplakia or other cancers of the throat and mouth. Going to the NIH would be like one-stop shopping, so to speak, and would give him a break from doctors.

He would be up to date for at least a year. He was willing to endure an extensive week of testing if he could just not have to think about Dyskeratosis Congenita for a little bit afterward.

I started the application process, and then we held our breaths to hear if we were accepted. If he was in, it meant that our family would most likely go through more than a million dollars of testing for free. The purpose of this kind of study is solely to advance scientific research, but the NIH is very gracious in sending all participants' results to any of their doctors who would like to have them.

We received the call that Brad was accepted in September 2014 and that our family would be going to the NIH in November. The timing was particularly fortunate because the NIH is operated by the federal government and in October 2014 funding for this study was stopped. No other participants were being accepted until further notice. We had gotten in just under the wire.

Our coordinator at the NIH was a godsend. She walked us through the myriad of details in the weeks leading up to our visit, during our visit, and — to this day — if we need anything, she is still there for us. Thank you, Maureen! You were our lifeline while we were in the vortex of the NIH study.

On Sunday, November 9, 2014 we were scheduled to fly to Baltimore. It was a tense day for all of us, but especially for Brad. He was going to be the focus of this intense microscope. We were all going to be lab rats, but Brad was the chief rat. He was particularly edgy. When Brad was upset, he got very prickly. We were waiting for our flight and having lunch.

"Yes, you've been dealt a sucky hand of cards. There's no doubt about it, but gifts come in strange ways," I said.

He could not believe what he was hearing.

"What do you mean by *gifts*?!" he asked.

I explained that as a family, and of course in particular with him, we had the gift of not knowing he had Dyskeratosis Congenita from birth. We had the gift of being a "normal" family for many years. As a child, he got to play little league, learn how to drive a car, go to prom, go to college — all the while not knowing he had this devastating disease. We had the gift of not spending his childhood running from one doctor's office to the other, since now he has at least eight different specialists he has to see. I told him that if we had known that he had Dyskeratosis Congenita from birth, I would have been a very different parent.

Brad looked at me, taking in the magnitude of what I had just told him, and gasped "You would have never let me be on the fire department for almost 10 years if you knew I had DC!"

"Gee, Brad, let's see — you have pulmonary fibrosis — *of course* I wouldn't have let you go into structure fires on an ongoing basis!"

The NIH put us up at a very accommodating hotel with two bedrooms, two bathrooms, a living room, dining area, and small kitchen. It was great for the four of us, since we were all a bit claustrophobic. We had our schedules sent to us prior to arrival and knew we were in for one hell of a week. Garrett was amazing, especially given the fact that he has OCD, which manifests itself in fear of self-harm. He was completely present and willing to do whatever was necessary for his brother. As anyone who is from a family where one family member has a devastating disease knows, it is not just the diagnosed patient who is affected, it truly is everyone, and each family member has their own way of coping — or not coping — with it.

We were scheduled to be at the NIH first thing Monday morning, and would be on the campus until 3 p.m. Friday afternoon. Each of us had a different schedule, but for the most part we endured many of the same tests and procedures, except for Brad. He had to deal with the most. As a family, we participated in 89 tests and procedures and donated 96 vials of blood. Brad donated 36 vials; the other three of us only 20 each. Included with Brad's many procedures was yet another bone marrow aspiration.

While we were at the NIH, we ran into someone from Canada I had met at Camp Sunshine. I believe he was in his late 40s, or maybe just 50 at the time, and was a participant in the NIH's study of the steroid Danazol. As part of the study, he received Danazol free of charge, and was having some success with the medication. Little did we know at that time that this drug would play an enormous part in Brad's later treatment.

It was great for Brad to meet another DC patient for the first time. He was very welcoming to Brad and offered his contact information if Brad ever wanted to reach out. That is what our Camp Sunshine family is like. While we were there, several other DCO board members were in Maryland for a genetic conference and they, too, offered support.

It was an intense week. At one point, during a pulmonary test, I had a band around my forehead with some sort of probe attached, and they had me walking briskly in circles. I felt like a lab rat.

When I had to have my bloodwork done, I had to lie high up on a pediatric table, because I'm a fainter. Lying there, I couldn't help but worry about Garrett having his blood done, because he has small veins that tend to collapse. I just kept imagining him being poked over and over and felt terrible, which made me want to faint even more. Brad, on the other hand, had no problem giving blood; he had seen a lot during his experience with the fire department and wasn't squeamish. Every time I would be with him in the hospital when he was having a bone marrow aspiration and they were prepping him for the procedure, he would love to try to make me faint, saying "Mom, look, look!" Brad had an impish sense of humor and a laugh to match, another thing we loved about him.

Even though we were in a nice hotel, had free shuttle service to and from the NIH, plus a generous daily food allowance in cash for each of us, this was anything but a vacation. But we did it. It was an unimaginable week, putting each of us through the ringer, but we endured. Bruce always says it is a testament to our family's bond that if we could endure that unbelievable week at the NIH, we could make it through anything.

We returned home one week before Thanksgiving. For years, we have hosted Bruce's entire family for Thanksgiving, with everyone arriving on Wednesday and departing on Saturday. It's a lot of work, but always worth it. Since I do all the cooking, and Bruce and I work on preparing the house for so many people, we bowed out of hosting this year, opting to spend the holiday alone at home with just the four of us. We needed it. We needed just an easy day. It is probably my most memorable of all the Thanksgivings we have ever had. The four of us just sat at the dining room table for almost three hours. I don't have a clue what we talked about, but the image is permanently etched in my mind. Tears are streaming down my face as I type this.

CHAPTER 6

This Can't Be Happening Again

With the holidays behind us, and Brad's Dyskeratosis Congenita, bone marrow failure, and pulmonary fibrosis in a holding pattern, we thought 2015 would be relatively smooth sailing, at least in terms of DC management for Brad. Little did we know what we were in for. All the results from the study went to all of our doctors, but specifically to Eva at DFCI, who received and reviewed everything.

She requested that Garrett have more bloodwork done and sent to her. I was traveling for work and was in Baltimore when I got her call. She started by saying she was very sorry to have to tell me this information over the phone — it really bothered her — but she had no choice since she was in Boston, I was in Maryland, and Bruce and Garrett were in Florida. Then she said that Garrett, too, had Dyskeratosis Congenita! I lost it. I went to my room, ordered wine, and bawled.

Bruce and I struggled about how and when to tell Garrett this devastating news. He, like Brad, was 25 when he was diagnosed. He is a deeply sensitive person who gives his all to all he cares for. We wanted to find the right time and the right way to tell him. Unfortunately, that's not what happened at all.

We had gone out to dinner, and Garrett and I were having our usual fun banter back and forth, when he suddenly said, "So I suppose I have DC, too."

"Yes," I said.

I've always been honest with each of our sons, but this just fell out. It wasn't the time and it clearly wasn't the place, and it wasn't the way we should have told him. I wanted to rewind the tape and have a "do over," but I couldn't. His face was heartbreaking. He was fighting back tears. How could this be? What are the odds of having two children with an extremely rare, highly fatal disease? Why us?

Well, we found out the answer quickly. As I mentioned before, we had met Dr. Suneet Agarwal from the Boston Children's Hospital, and Brad was already part of his genetic study. Suneet is also a medical advisor for DCO, and we are able to talk when we're at Camp. Suneet asked if Garrett would also be part of his DC genetic study. After getting over the shock of his diagnosis, Garrett agreed to be a participant. This meant that Garrett, as the patient, would have to do certain tests, and that all three of us had to do more bloodwork and have the samples overnighted back to Boston. Suneet put the bloodwork through his study and called us. He explained that Bruce and I each have a rare genetic mutation — but not the same one — and that one of them is rarer than the other. When you put Bruce's and my DNA together it results in the "PARN" genetic mutation for Dyskeratosis Congenita. This means Brad and Garrett are what is called Autosomal Recessive. They have the mutation because Bruce and I each contributed a mutated gene to them.

As a parent, you feel so responsible because it's your DNA that has contributed to your children's DNA, but you must let that go. Neither Bruce nor I blame ourselves, or each other, and we are a united front when it comes to this issue. Obviously, we had no way of knowing. Had we known, would we have chosen to have children? That is something we will never know; but what Bruce and I do know is that we cannot imagine ever not having Brad and Garrett in our lives. They have brought us so much joy. History cannot be rewritten. It is what it is. What can be done going forward is how we choose to navigate through this hellish sea of doctors, testing, and treatments. In the end, we would turn over every stone to seek out the latest information on Dyskeratosis Congenita for our sons. We would not settle for okay. We would seek out the best knowledge available, and do whatever we could to be certain they would get the best treatments possible.

When I attended my first retreat at Camp Sunshine in 2012, only nine genetic DC mutations had been discovered. By the time I attended my third retreat in September of 2016, 13 mutations had been found. The discovery of four new mutations in four short years shows real progress in DC research. As a DC family, we are indebted to the passion, commitment, and dedication of the doctors who aggressively and continually work toward understanding Dyskeratosis Congenita.

This book is not meant to be a clinical guide to Dyskeratosis Congenita, only a brief synopsis of what it means to our family.

When I started writing this, I said that being one in a million, being rare, being unique, is not always a great thing. Yes, it is great to know your specific mutation when diagnosed with a rare genetic disease — many DC patients never learn of theirs — but it can also be a double-edged sword. Brad and Garrett's mutation is called PARN. Many other DC patients, but not all, have either the TERC or TERT mutation. When Garrett and I went to meet with Eva and Lisa Brennan at DFCI, Eva told us that, to date, there was only one other patient in the world who had been diagnosed with the PARN mutation. *What?* She also said that since Brad and Garrett were patients "2 and 3" in the world with the PARN mutation it meant that we have no way of knowing how their Dyskeratosis Congenita was going to progress. She also said that Brad's and Garrett's Dyskeratosis Congenita was already progressing differently, so again, we couldn't predict anything at this point. Great! Seriously!

Later, during Camp in September 2016, Dr. Alison Bertuch, from the Baylor College of Medicine in Houston, Texas, said that she had two other patients with the PARN mutation.

So, what does a DC mutation mean for patients? Well, in layman's terms, it means that, depending on the mutation, a patient may or may not have all the traits of the disease, or may have the same traits, but to a different degree.

Shortly after Garrett's diagnosis he moved back home to Florida for a brief time, to save some money and decide where he wanted to live and look for a new job. We were thrilled to have him with us, especially since he had just been diagnosed, and we didn't want him to be alone to digest this difficult information.

Brad's medical support team was well established between Portland and Boston. Now we had the task of trying to do this for Garrett in the Port St. Lucie, Florida area. This proved to be an impossible task. We spoke to Eva about a referral for a hematologist in the area. She talked with a colleague at Shands Hospital in Gainesville, Florida. The news wasn't good, although he said there was one doctor in the area that we might try. We contacted that office, but it took six weeks to get Garrett's files sent from his primary care provider, the DFCI, and the NIH. After a few more weeks, we called to see if this doctor would accept him as a new patient. She said no, because Garrett didn't have cancer yet. *What!?* Could this be for real? Continually monitoring CBCs for DC patients is critical, but this doctor was saying she wouldn't do it. Why not? We just couldn't understand her logic. Garrett already had an extremely rare, highly fatal genetic disease, which hadn't yet manifested into a cancer. Wasn't that enough to qualify for care?

Even his primary care doctor in this city was terrible. When we first met with her, we arrived armed with as much information about Dyskeratosis Congenita as we had at the time. She said she understood about Dyskeratosis Congenita, but there was no follow through on her part. She did take the time once to speak with Eva, but that appeared to be pretty much the extent of her interest.

Nevertheless, we sort of settled in with Garrett's "medical team" as best as we could, since he was in transition. Once he decided where he wanted to go, we could do the research and find a more suitable team where he eventually moved. Since he was trying to get a job writing for the gaming industry, he thought being closer to his college would be a good idea, so he moved back to the Orlando, Florida area.

We started to research doctors who might be a good fit for Garrett's needs again. With Eva's help, we were able to find a hematologist we were all comfortable with, and, to our relief, this hematologist accepted Garrett as a patient. Garrett established a good relationship with this doctor who also helped with a recommendation for a primary care physician. Having at least those two doctors in place was comforting to all of us. His hematologist was very good about communicating to Eva at DFCI, which was also extremely reassuring.

We were able to find several other doctors for Garrett, but one more he needed was a good psychiatrist, to help manage his OCD and depression. Unfortunately, this doctor turned out to be a nightmare, because she was both impossible to see and would not refill prescriptions unless she saw him. As a result, Garrett's meds would often run out, which had major consequences for him.

We decided that Garrett should go back to DFCI to meet with Eva. We wanted both Brad and Garrett to have the same oncologist, so that even though all their other doctors would be different, their medical information would all be funneled to the same home base. Eva is amazing! She is thorough and direct, and has a tremendous amount of compassion. She genuinely cares about her patients. She takes the time to communicate, often and in every way possible. I can send her an email, and often I get a response immediately. We have even received calls on a Sunday night!

At this point, Garrett was in a monitoring pattern, with nothing especially urgent going on. Brad's numbers from his CBCs were trending lower, however.

In January 2015, Brad and I went back to DFCI for a follow up. They suggested that Brad might want to consider starting the search for a bone marrow donor. DC patients' numbers trend at their own rate, but one thing I believe they all have in common is that the numbers never really go up. They may teeter, but usually the teetering is only temporary. Since his numbers were trending lower, starting a search before the numbers got very low and he became very, very sick would be a wise thing to do.

YOU WON'T BELIEVE IT (BUT IT'S TRUE)

CHAPTER 7

Trying to Find a Match

Brad agreed to start the search for a donor. He wanted to go forward with a bone marrow transplant. He asked Eva to begin the search and put feelers out to see who in the Boston area would consider going through a transplant with Brad. The news we heard back was heartbreaking. Brigham and Women's Hospital in Boston didn't exactly say no, but with Brad's risk factors — bone marrow failure, pulmonary fibrosis, and liver fibrosis — he was too high risk for transplant, and they didn't want to do it. DFCI basically said that if "push came to shove" they would, but they, too, didn't want to do it because Brad was so high risk. So now what?

Again, Camp Sunshine comes into play. When I attended that first 2012 retreat, there were two doctors who specialized in performing bone marrow transplants in DC patients. One doctor was located at the Children's Hospital in Los Angeles; the other was at the University of Minnesota Hospital. I wrote down those two doctors' names and contact information, because even though I did not know we were facing transplant that September, I knew that we would be going down that road at some point. Unfortunately.

Because the DC world is so small, all the doctors who are well versed in the disease tend to know each other. When Eva gave us the news that Boston didn't look like an option, she also mentioned Dr. Andrew Dietz in Los Angeles and Dr. Jakub Tolar at the University of Minnesota.

One of the many, many things we have learned about Dyskeratosis Congenita is that when it comes to the doctors who treat DC patients, or any other major illnesses, there is a pediatric and an adult "side" for treatment. This is also the case when it comes to bone marrow transplants. Since Dr. Dietz was known for his pediatric work at the Children's Hospital, we decided to contact Dr. Tolar. But we learned that he, too, is on the pediatric side of bone marrow transplants. When I contacted the University of Minnesota through their website and requested an appointment with Dr. Tolar, the first thing they asked was Brad's age. He was 28. They told us that Brad was not eligible to see Dr. Tolar, but would be transferred to Dr. Brian McClune, head of the adult side of transplant.

All of Brad's records were sent to Dr. McClune, and he agreed to see him.

Brad and I flew to Minnesota in June 2015 to see if he could be accepted for transplant. This was going to be an intense visit, so I was trying everything possible to have a few light moments peppered in between the intensity, so we saw the Red Sox play the Twins at Target Field and went to The Mall of America. (For baseball fans, Target Field is a great place to watch a game. As for the mall, it's just a large mall with a redundancy of stores.)

The University of Minnesota Hospital campus is quite large and Dr. McClune's office was in a brand new building. Brad was checked in but anxious. To make matters worse, Dr. McClune was running late, which only added to Brad's anxiety. When we finally were able to meet Dr. McClune, he sat with us for an hour and a half and explained how a bone marrow transplant works.

As anyone can imagine, a bone marrow transplant is no day at the park. Transplant "days" all count and have great significance. But before the transplant clock can even start, the donor match must be calculated. Depending on the disease and/or patient, doctors prefer to have what they call an 8- or 10-point match. This means that the donor and receiver have to match on eight or ten critical points before a transplant can even be considered.

With every point not met (e.g., 7 out of 8, or 9 out of 10 and so on), there is an added chance of Graft Versus Host Disease (GVHD). GVHD varies in range and poses real threats to patients, possibly claiming their lives.

∽

T(Transplant) minus 10:

Ten days prior to transplant the patient is given an intense "cocktail" of drugs to erase the patient's immune system. When I say erase, I mean eradicate. Gone. So much so, that if a patient survives transplant, at some point they have to have all of their immunizations over again, just like they were newborn babies.

Once the patient makes it to "T"- Transplant, and not all patients make it through to this stage, then the transplant itself occurs intravenously. This seems to be the easiest part. It takes between approximately one to a few hours and is relatively painless for the recipient, initially. At this point, it's the bone marrow donor who experiences most of the pain, however. A bone marrow transplant requires approximately a one-liter soda bottle of bone marrow to be donated. This means that the matching donor must undergo between 50 and 100 bone marrow aspirations in one procedure, under anesthesia. Their pelvic regions are pummeled with huge syringes 50 to 100 times until enough marrow has been collected. Bone marrow donors are truly unsung heroes!

There is also a peripheral blood stem cell transplantation, which is a completely different collection protocol, but offers another option for the donor and patient. At this point, we were not looking down that path for Brad.

Once the transplant is completed, then the intense "100-day countdown" period begins. The goal is to be able to release the patient from the hospital between about day 30 to 45, with very close monitoring after that. It is during this time when the recipient's body will naturally try to reject the bone marrow donation. The body is saying "whoa," you don't belong here. This process of rejection is unpredictable and very risky. In terms of other issues at the same time, some patients experience few GVHD symptoms, while others have many more. GVHD symptoms range from rashes; blistering of exposed skin; nausea, vomiting, abdominal cramps, and diarrhea; loss of appetite; jaundice, because of effects on the liver; excessive dryness of the mouth and throat; and dryness of lungs, vagina, and other surfaces. The severity of GVHD varies from patient to patient.

If the patient accepts the stem cells; recovers their blood counts; and is relatively free of GVHD, infections, or other problems, they can be released from the hospital. If not, more time in the hospital may be needed. Once the patient is released from the hospital, they are still monitored very closely in the clinic — either daily or several times a week. Throughout this time, the patient's family may be placed in a hospital-affiliated housing facility to be near their loved ones through this very difficult process. There are stages of release in slowly getting the patient out of quarantine to everyday normal life, often taking more than a year, with strictly-scheduled return follow up visits for years thereafter.

We sat on the edge of our seats and listened to Dr. McClune tell us the reality of transplant. With this illness, we continue to learn medical information that we never, in our wildest dreams, would ever think we would need to know.

Brad still wanted to go to transplant so, Dr. McClune now moved his donor search from New England to Minnesota. The initial search found a few 7-out-of-8 matches. We thought, great, looking in Minnesota was getting us close enough. But much to our great disappointment it turned out that, given Brad's risk factors, it wasn't enough. Going into transplant without an 8 out of 8-point match would make Brad's risks even greater. The bone marrow registry continued looking for the right match.

CHAPTER 8

Management and Monitoring Challenges, Times Two

Two sons with a rare genetic disease was a challenge for the whole family. At this point, both Brad and Garrett had an average of 10 doctors they needed to see. We made charts with each doctor's category in its own column, with contact information and how often they needed to be seen to help keep track of which patient saw which doctor on which schedule.

The list of specialists is daunting:

- Primary Care Physician
- Oncologist
- Hematologist
- Pulmonologist
- Ophthalmologist
- Dermatologist
- ENT Specialist
- Dentist
- Urologist
- Hepatologist

Often many adult patients also have a therapist to help them navigate through these very muddy waters.

Along with all the doctors to be seen, DC patients also need to have regular CBCs, and at least one yearly bone marrow aspiration to monitor the degree of bone marrow failure or — hopefully — lack thereof.

This monitoring is taxing, regardless of the patient's age. They are tired of being poked and prodded, especially the young patients and young adults. They are sick and tired of hearing their results, which typically never get better. The news is almost never good, and they just want to be healthy. They want to be able to do normal things. Just being out in the sun is a challenge for DC patients, since they are so prone to skin cancers. Special clothing with high SPF values is recommended; not wearing sunscreen is never an option.

Garrett had recently moved back home with us again to save some money and give himself time to decide "what's next." This meant finding yet another new medical support team. But this time was going to be different. After all he had been through, there was no way that I was going to let his medical care fall through the cracks in our part of Florida. While trying to "sift" out good doctors from the ones would not be a good fit for Garrett, I actually had a doctor tell me that "the area we lived in was the medical armpit of the state of Florida!" I couldn't believe what I was hearing!

Thankfully, a group of women I was golfing with one day began talking about the lack of strong medical care in the area. One woman said we might have better luck in a different city. Finally, a ray of hope. It wasn't easy, but I kept researching and began finding a medical support team that could be the right fit for Garrett.

I am grateful for golf, by the way. It gives me two hours a couple of times a week when I don't think about Dyskeratosis Congenita. Although, if a fellow golfer asks about the boys' health, my mind drifts back to it and my game goes to hell, not that it's ever very good. I always appreciate it when someone asks, though, because most people are afraid to talk about it. We know it is too much to comprehend and, if you're not living it, too much to process.

I've also taken up bowling and for an hour or two each week. I can release a ton of frustration by smacking the heck out of those ten little pins!

After Garrett moved back home, he needed a new baseline with each doctor. Along with many cancers, leukemias, bone marrow failure, and pulmonary fibrosis, DC patients can have problems with their eyesight and can even go blind. Seeing an ophthalmologist who is a retinal specialist at least once is recommended in order to establish a baseline. Bruce is type one diabetic and his eye care is extremely important. His specialist in Maine referred him to a retinal specialist in Florida whom he really likes, so we felt comfortable trying to set Garrett up with him as well.

Well, it wasn't that easy. The receptionist who answered my call argued with me that Garrett did not need an ophthalmologist. Once again, I had to put the DC "PhD" hat back on and educate one more person about why we wanted our son to be seen by this particular doctor.

"Fine, I'll make the appointment for your son, but if, after the exam the results show that he doesn't need this type of doctor, he'll no longer be a patient and will have to find an optometrist!" she said.

A receptionist was "diagnosing" our son based on nothing! She didn't have a clue about DC, and didn't seem to care.

It turned out this doctor was exactly the right fit for Garrett. He was diagnosed with Lattice Degeneration, which means the sun can severely damage his eyes. He has to wear 100% UV lenses at all times and will be this retinal specialist's patient from now on.

CHAPTER 9

Let's Make Things Harder — aka Health Insurance!

I want to tell you about some of the battles we've had with health insurance since we began navigating this disease.

For starters, once Brad was diagnosed it was imperative that he have genetic testing to see if we could determine his exact genetic mutation. At the time, the only place that did this type of testing was in Vancouver, Canada. Before we agreed to have the testing done, we checked with our insurance company to be certain that it was covered. We were told it was, so we went ahead. Two weeks before Christmas, we received an Explanation of Benefits (EOB) stating that the testing was not medically necessary and that Blue Cross Blue Shield would not pay any part of the $18,000 bill. I broke down in tears. Garrett happened to be home when I opened the mail and when I burst into tears, he immediately hugged me and started to cry himself. He could see the pain in my face. My hands were trembling while I kept re-reading the EOB. I called Blue Cross Blue Shield right away and lost it on some poor person who had the misfortune of taking my call and hearing the angst and wrath in my voice. Eventually, the claim was processed properly and the bill was completely covered, but challenging EOBs have become a routine thing for us.

Then Brad had to have surgery for yet another urethral stricture. However, this surgery was much different than his previous eight or nine dilations, and he would need to have reconstructive surgery of the urethral passage. This is a difficult surgery to begin with, but with Brad's risk factors it was very high risk. Since Brad's CBCs were so low, his surgeon postponed the surgery and required Brad to take Danazol, a steroid known to temporarily elevate his numbers. This is the same drug that the DC patient from Canada we met during the NIH study was taking. Once Brad was on this medication, new blood work would be drawn, and if he could get his platelets to at least 30,000, the surgery could be performed — with a platelet transfusion on hand — so that Brad would not risk bleeding to death on the operating table.

Blue Cross Blue Shield, once again, denied this claim, stating that Danazol was not covered because Brad did not have fibrous breast tissue, endometriosis, or severe edema. That's correct — our son does not have breasts, a uterus, or ovaries! However, the NIH and the New England Journal of Medicine (NEJM) had completed studies on using Danazol for DC patients and the benefits it gave them. Brad's doctors at DFCI, The University of Minnesota, and the Lahey Clinic in Burlington, Massachusetts all wanted him on this medication. We appealed the EOB. Blue Cross Blue Shield upheld the decision to deny the claim. We could not believe what we were hearing. I was on edge waiting for the appeal decision and was in a restaurant when I got the call. I went ballistic! I broke into tears and was yelling at the person who was telling me Blue Cross Blue Shield's decision. Some clerk, sitting behind a keyboard while looking at our claim, must have checked a manual and since this usage of Danazol was not in it, they denied it. Plain and simple. We had submitted our doctors' letters and the NIH and NEJM studies with the appeal, but they still denied it!

We were determined not to settle for this answer and continued to fight. We learned that each state has a Commissioner of Insurance Office. Every single consumer has the right to plead his or her case to the Commissioner. You plead your case online and after filling in all the required fields, consumers are allowed 4,000 characters (about 500 words) to explain why they are challenging a claim's decision.

I used every single character, choosing my words carefully. I explained the devastation of Dyskeratosis Congenita. I explained that with every passing day that Brad did not have Danazol, his urethral stricture was worsening and could eventually rupture or cause his kidneys to double in size and/or burst. I asked Blue Cross Blue Shield if they were willing to be responsible for either of those outcomes.

I wrote that, as patients, it's our responsibility to take whatever preventive measures possible to avoid more serious conditions. By denying Brad the medication he needed, they were being irresponsible. I also said that, as devastating as Dyskeratosis Congenita is, in our case having two sons with the disease meant that at some point it was likely that Garrett would need Danazol, too, and that it would be unbearable to think both of our sons would be denied the only medication that is able to help their CBCs, even in the short term. How could Blue Cross Blue Shield conscionably make such a decision?

Along with our appeal, our doctors wrote letters again, and Eva was actually on the phone with Blue Cross Blue Shield for two hours fighting for Brad. We were given a case number and an assigned case worker. She was very calming, which was exactly what I needed since my head felt like it was going to pop off my shoulders.

We were told that once they had all of our documentation, Blue Cross Blue Shield had a certain amount of time to submit their entire case to the Commissioner's office. Once everything was collected and in order, our case would go to a blind, independent team of "like" doctors. This scared me. I immediately asked how could they reassure us that they were "like" doctors when most of the medical community is unaware of Dyskeratosis Congenita? They said they had no control over who the review team would be. Legally, they have to stay neutral. We understood, but were freaking out because it could be another week before we knew. Another week that Brad was not on the medicine he so desperately needed.

Friday morning, January 13, we received a call from the Commissioner's office. It was our case worker. She said that Blue Cross Blue Shield had reversed their decision and finally approved the Danazol, that the case was closed, and it would not be going to the blind, independent panel of doctors! We fought a major medical insurance company and won! We don't know if this is an individual win, but we hope that if any other DC patient needs Danazol, this case has helped open the doors for them.

These are just two examples of what seemed like weekly battles with claims deemed "medically unnecessary" and denied because of how rare Dyskeratosis Congenita is and the lack of knowledge about it in the medical community. I keep reiterating this, but I need to. Every chance we, as DC patients and families, have to educate the medical community of Dyskeratosis Congenita helps. Baby steps, but hopefully they all lead to something positive.

Back to Brad. His prescription was finally approved, so he went to the pharmacy to pick it up. It was denied again! This couldn't be happening! Brad called me and was completely pissed off. I immediately called our case worker. The pharmacy had made a clerical error. Someone had typed in the wrong code! *Uncle!!!* Finally, the prescription was filled. Brad was finally on his way to finding out if this drug would help his numbers enough so that he could make it to surgery. He took the Danazol for 30 days, then had blood work. His platelet count was at 30,000. Surgery was rescheduled for March 16.

CHAPTER 10

Something No Young Man Should Have to Endure

I was scheduled to arrive in Maine on Monday, March 13, 2017. Bruce is a weather enthusiast, always following the weather, especially if one of us is traveling. He recommended I change my flight and fly out on Sunday instead. I appreciated his recommendation and did just that. I flew into Maine on Sunday; it was 42 degrees when I landed. I was staying at a hotel in South Portland, directly across from the Maine Mall. I checked in and then headed straight to Macy's to get some appropriate attire, since I was coming from Florida's 90-degree heat. This turned out to be a smart move. Monday through Tuesday, Maine was hit by a nor'easter. The snow was falling sideways and was so dense you literally could not see the mall!

We rode out the storm, Brad picked me up at the hotel on Wednesday, and we drove to our hotel in Burlington, Massachusetts, close to the Lahey Clinic. Brad was tense. He chose to stay in the room for the night. I went to the restaurant to have dinner; he ordered room service.

The day of surgery we left the hotel in the dark — it was only 5 a.m. Brad's was the first surgery of the day, so he needed to be there very early. It was interesting to see him being intense and calm at the same time. He reminded me of myself, on my wedding day. You know there's a life-changing event about to happen, you don't know the outcome, but you know it's the right thing to do. A strange calm comes over you.

Brad began talking about an inventory of things that needed to be done at Sugarloaf. Dishes in the sink, an extra load of laundry... He loved our place there and took great pride in caring for it, now that he was its winter resident. He didn't want me to be surprised or upset walking into the house and finding that certain things still needed to be done, especially since that was where his recovery would be taking place. He needed to be sure I knew before surgery. I understood.

By now we were at the Lahey Clinic. Brad was being prepped for surgery. Anxiety was high. Dr. Alex Vanni was not pleased and had almost cancelled surgery because Brad had missed one of his pre-op appointments. He also said that no doctor would want to do this surgery, because Brad was so high risk. He also told Brad, in no uncertain terms, that he had to do post-op care by the book. Period. Recovery would be hard. No lifting, bending, stairs for four weeks, etc.

Brad and I had a brief moment alone before they wheeled him off to surgery. He asked me if I thought he was going to bleed to death on the table. I told him I didn't know, but certainly hoped he wouldn't. As they were taking him to surgery, I told him I loved him.

"Mom, I love you too," he said.

With Brad in surgery, I headed for one of the waiting areas in the clinic. I hadn't eaten anything yet and tried to eat, but I began to have an anxiety attack. The months of worrying about the surgery and now the reality of all the risks involved were hitting me hard. I thought someone might have to roll me into the ER and start testing me for a heart attack. After about 30 minutes it finally subsided.

Waiting was brutal. Even though many people offered to sit with me, I was glad, in an odd way, to be alone. When things are very tense for me, I internalize and shut down. Small talk isn't an option. I probably would have snapped.

Finally, after four hours, Dr. Vanni and an assistant came to find me. He told me Brad was in recovery. There had been excessive bleeding, but the platelet transfusion had helped. He said Brad's stricture had been 100% blocked. It was the worst one he had ever seen and he could not figure out how he was able to void at all. But he felt that if Brad followed his recovery instructions, the surgery would be a complete success. Brad actually had two surgeries that day — urethral reconstructive surgery for a four-inch blockage, plus oral surgery to get the skin graft needed for the reconstructive surgery. Recovery was going to be very hard for him.

Once I had Dr. Vanni's update I called Bruce immediately. As I was telling him the outcome, my body started to shake all over and I couldn't stop crying. Again, it was the six months of bottled up worrying and struggle to get Brad to surgery. I was so glad he made it through surgery. There had been real risks of him not making it. I was so grateful for so many reasons.

I felt very bad for Bruce, because I knew he wanted to be at the clinic with me. But during this same time Garrett's OCD and depression medications were not being correctly addressed. The doctors kept changing his meds, with severe consequences. Some of the meds were giving him suicidal thoughts. Bruce and I had made the decision to divide and conquer. I would be with Brad at the hospital and during recovery. Bruce would stay with Garrett, so he would not be alone and would make sure his team of doctors kept plugging along until they got him the right help.

Brad had to stay in the hospital overnight. I was grateful for that. I did not want the responsibility of trying to get him the proper care if there were any repercussions from the surgery. He was in good hands there. I went back to the hotel, ate, and then went to my room to collapse. Tomorrow I would find out how his first post-operative hours went.

When I arrived at the hospital the next morning, Brad was still asleep. He didn't seem comfortable. Even though your child is an adult, as a parent it is still gut wrenching to see that child in pain, and it is hard to know that there is nothing you can do about it. Oh, how I wished our kids didn't have this god-forsaken disease and all the ramifications that go with it!!! Hell, I just wanted them to have a normal life. Not one filled with doctors' appointments, tests, and procedures on their freaking calendars. To watch Brad hooked up to IVs, etc., to watch him try to move just a little to get comfortable, but see the pain on his face was almost unbearable. Though at this point I can almost hear Brad saying, "Geeze Mom, cut the theatrics, it wasn't that bad."

But it was bad for me. As I said before, "people can't do what they don't know." Neither of our sons could know the pain Bruce and I were trying to manage while watching them endure the realities of a rare genetic disease. A parent's pain is unique. Only another parent can relate to that.

We weren't sure if Brad was going to be released on Friday or not. It was wait and see, based on a few variables. Finally, around 3 p.m., we were told he could go home. I wasn't exactly happy about this new information because we had to drive almost five hours to Sugarloaf in Carrabassett Valley, Maine. Once we got to our place at Sugarloaf, we would be up in the remote western mountains of Maine. The nearest hospital is an hour away, down a winding mountain road that runs parallel to the Carrabassett Valley River — a challenging road, even on good weather days. In bad conditions, this road is treacherous. My biggest fear was that if Brad started to bleed excessively, I would have to try to get him down the mountain. God forbid if it was snowing or there was an ice storm. I had talked to Bruce about this extensively, and he knew it was freaking me out. We talked about options and decided I would keep the number of the Carrabassett Valley Fire Department in my phone, with a contact name. I would explain our situation and have them on alert, so they could transport him to the hospital if necessary. Hell, I didn't care if they needed to life flight him down the mountain, but I wasn't going to let anything happen to Brad on my watch. Especially after all it took just to get him into surgery.

We finally left the hospital a little after 4 p.m. This meant driving most of the way in the dark, which makes the ride up the mountain even more challenging. Brad was hooked up to a catheter and bag and was visibly uncomfortable. He had a special air pad to help with the pain. We also had to stop at his pharmacy in Maine to get more Danazol. Thankfully, the rest of his meds were filled right at the hospital.

For those who don't travel or know about Maine roads in winter, the expression "you're in for a bumpy ride" is perfect. Rapidly changing temperatures mean that Maine roads are known for their frost heaves in winter, making driving on most of them literally like being on a roller coaster. Some of the frost heaves are so severe you can go airborne if you are driving too fast when you hit them. Also, they sort of "pop up" on you. This made the ride for Brad even more challenging. The closer we got to home, the more intense the frost heaves were. I kept trying to brace for them to make it as comfortable as possible, but that was impossible. Poor Brad, he groaned and said just keep going. He wanted to get out of the damn car!

We did it! We made it to the house and got Brad inside. Once he was settled, I had to unload the car and get everything upstairs. We got to the house at 9 p.m.; I didn't sit down until 10:30. I was exhausted, but it was Brad doing all the really hard work.

I have to say a huge thank you here. While we were in pre-op on Thursday morning, it occurred to me that it had snowed at Sugarloaf. Great! Now I would have to figure out how to get the entry shoveled before we got up there, so Brad would not fall trying to get in the house. I texted Ross and Ricky, two of Brad's closest friends, who just recently bought their own house there. They immediately texted me back and said they would take care of it. I appreciated this so much! Then it dawned on me that if Brad were released on Friday, the guys wouldn't be able to shovel the entryway in time, since they work at least until 5 p.m., and then have to factor in their own travel time to get up there. So I called Foster, who does our yearly plowing there. I explained our situation and he asked if Friday morning would be too late. It wasn't. When we arrived Friday night, Foster had not only plowed as close to the house as possible, he had even shoveled the front steps. I don't think he ever charged us. On Saturday, Ross, Ricky, and their friend Nick all showed up and shoveled the upper deck for me. I appreciated all this so much more than I can say. Thank you, guys!!!

Now the recovery began. Brad was on a regimen of meds. Danazol to keep his numbers up, pain meds, and antibiotics. He was in pain from the reconstructive surgery, as well as the oral surgery. One can only imagine the pain. Through all of it, he was amazing. He never complained. He was a model patient, and did everything as instructed. For the first ten or so days he stayed downstairs. Eventually he attacked the steps. He never overdid it. He was also so appreciative of all that I was doing to help him recover.

We left Sugarloaf 18 days later and headed back to Burlington. We stayed in the same hotel as the previous time and headed back to the Lahey Clinic the next morning for the catheter removal. In the end, all went well. Then Brad and I headed back to Maine.

Brad's pleasant demeanor returned on that drive. It was nice to have him back. We stopped for lunch at a place we liked in Kittery. He was so glad to be done with the surgery and to be able to walk without anything attached to him. He had a cocktail and oysters, his favorite. It was the home opener for the Red Sox! We ate, watched Boston, and laughed. At the end of the meal, Brad grabbed the check and said "for all you did for me and the hell you went through, this one's on me." It really meant a lot and took me by surprise, because you do what you need to for your children, regardless of their age. A "thank you" from him had never crossed my mind. Again, it really meant a lot.

One month after Brad's surgery he went back to see his urologist. The surgery had been a complete success! Even though it had been very high risk, it was extremely necessary, and hopefully its success would take at least one DC issue off of his plate permanently.

CHAPTER 11

Ego, Condescension, and Frustration — The Camel's Back

As I've described, setting up Garrett's new team of specialists in Florida was quite difficult; however, we finally felt we had a team that was qualified and would work well with Eva at DFCI. Garrett was due for his annual bone marrow aspiration at a clinic that is about an hour from our home. His aspiration was scheduled for the third week in May. Garrett was anxious as we drove there; we checked in, and sat in the waiting room for an unusually long period of time. We kept checking the time. We should have been called in at least 15 minutes ago. *Hmmm.* What was going on?

Finally, a woman opened the door to the waiting room area and called Garrett's name. We rose.

"Well, you're not going to like this, but it's not happening today," she said. "Follow me."

What? We were ushered into a room and waited for his doctor to come in and explain exactly what, or should I say wasn't, happening today.

The doctor told us that they knew yesterday that Garrett's bone marrow aspiration wasn't going to take place today because the only person who could assist him couldn't make it in today. At this point

I snapped! Could I actually be hearing this correctly? They KNEW yesterday and didn't think to call us! My advocate hat was strapped on tight at this point.

"Excuse me, but you knew yesterday and no one thought to call us?!?" I said. "Our time is just as valuable as yours is, doctor. Having two sons with this devastating disease, we have to manage 20 specialists and are constantly managing appointments. Getting to this appointment is a two-hour round trip. Garrett is already anxious and now it's not happening! This is unprofessional!"

The doctor started to ask some questions, but my advocacy hat was strapped on for quite a ride at this point! I asked to interject a couple of questions.

"So, doctor, we know there are three schools of thought regarding how to do a bone marrow aspiration: under general anesthesia, with mild sedative and numbing agent, or just the numbing agent without anything to calm the patient. What is your method?"

He asked Garrett how his first aspiration was administered, which was with just the numbing and no sedative. He asked Garrett if that would be okay. Garrett said yes, but I knew it was with reluctance. Then the doctor turned to me.

"Well, Garrett is okay with it. Have *you* ever had a bone marrow aspiration?" he said.

It took all my energy not to leap out of my chair and throttle this man! How dare he! I have zero tolerance for condescension. The doctor went on to say we would reschedule the procedure for some time in June. This was the straw that broke the proverbial camel's back. I stood up.

"No, we won't," I said. "I am leaving for Maine on Friday, May 26. We need to schedule this while I am still here. There is no way I want Garrett to have this procedure alone and, should something go wrong, I do not want him driving back for an hour by himself."

The procedure was rescheduled for May 23.

On the day of the procedure the doctor apologized to us profusely, and said that he and his staff had discussed the entire situation. They realized that they should have handled it differently and that they had learned from it. I appreciated the apology a great deal.

When Garrett was in the room alone with the doctor just before the test, he apologized again, and said that he appreciated the fact that Garrett didn't hold it against him. He also said he was not used to, or comfortable with confrontation, and that his own mom really came at him. Again, as parents we have to keep fighting the fight to be certain our children are not swept under the rug, mistreated, or not getting what is best for them.

It turned out there was a complication with clotting during the procedure and the aspiration had to be done twice. Poor Garrett could barely walk to the car. My heart broke for him. He was such a trooper and wouldn't complain, but you could see the pain on his face.

CHAPTER 12

June, 2017 – The Bottom Falls Out Again

Bruce was still in Florida, and I was at our home in Sugarloaf. It was a Wednesday and Eva had left me a voice mail, a text, and an email saying she needed to go over Garrett's most recent bone marrow aspiration results. She left a very specific window of time when she would call. This couldn't be good.

I immediately called Bruce. If there were no problems with the results she would have said so. I was pacing. Waiting for that phone call was torture.

When my cell phone rang, I was seated at the dining room table with pen and paper at the ready. It felt as if she was talking too fast. She wasn't. She was just giving us information that we hadn't seen coming at all.

First, she said that we all have 23 sets of chromosomes. Yes, I knew that, but beyond this, I must be honest, my knowledge is limited. She went on to tell me that sets 1 and 7 for Garrett were damaged and that set 7 was partially missing. She said that if 7 disappeared entirely we would be in big trouble and Garrett would become very sick.

She also told me that everyone's blood changes, all day every day. When cytogenetic results come in there can be what are called abnormalities or "flags." It is very common that any one of us on any given day can have one "flag." Doctors would pay attention to this, but they would not be on high alert. Patients with two "flags" would make doctors take a closer look. But when a patient has three or more "flags," it means that something is wrong.

We were told that Garrett had three clonal cytogenetic abnormalities, markers that could lead to Acute Myeloid Leukemia (AML). This was becoming too much. How on earth were we going to be able to tell Garrett this, too? Just days earlier, Garrett had asked Bruce to ask me to not give him any more test results. He couldn't take it, especially since he was not out of the woods with his mental health. Given his OCD, this type of information puts him in a repetitive tailspin.

Bruce and I talked a lot that night about how to approach this. We couldn't keep it from him, that would be irresponsible. But at the same time, he was freaking out and didn't want to hear it.

The next morning, when Garrett got up, Bruce asked him.

"We have your results from your bone marrow aspiration. Do you want to hear them?"

Garrett mustered the courage and said yes. As Bruce explained the results, he didn't say anything, but a tear was silently running down his cheek. That image still brings me to tears, even as I write.

CHAPTER 13

False Hope

Bruce and I were at Sugarloaf for the summer again, but this year was different because we had finally found a small condo in Brunswick that would be our new place to be in non-winter months. One morning I was at the gym on the treadmill watching something on Netflix to pass the time. A phone call rang through. The number was from Minnesota. My heart stopped beating! This was the University of Minnesota calling us with a bone marrow donor match for Brad! I stopped exercising and took the call.

I said hello, but there was a pause.

"Hello? Hello?" I said again.

It was a telemarketer. I didn't realize just how badly we were waiting for that call until it didn't come. I was shattered.

YOU WON'T BELIEVE IT (BUT IT'S TRUE)

CHAPTER 14

"Routine" Checkups (Hardly)

Since we now knew that Garrett is genetically wired for AML, Eva thought it was imperative that we make another trip to DFCI to discuss a bone marrow transplant for him. Both of our sons were facing high risk bone marrow transplants — what are the odds? Well, as I've said, less than one in a million!

Brad was also a little overdue to check in with Eva, so we decided that Brad, Garrett, and I would make the trip to Boston while Bruce stayed behind to take care of our dog Birdie and Garrett's cat Xena. Brad and Garrett each had an appointment with her, and hopefully Suneet, first thing Monday morning, August 7. Garrett was traveling from Florida, so he flew into Boston Sunday evening. Brad and I were traveling from different locations in Maine, so we decided to meet at the Double Tree Hotel in South Portland. I left my car in the hotel parking lot and Brad drove us into Boston. We were staying at the Westin Hotel in Back Bay.

The trip to Boston was terrible. Those of you who know what it's like to travel into and out of Maine on a summer weekend can appreciate why Mainers avoid it at all costs. Typically, going into Maine on Fridays and heading out of Maine on Sundays are nightmares when approaching the toll booth on I-95. God forbid if it's a holiday weekend! It can take hours of moving one mile per hour! We've had guests from Massachusetts visiting over the Fourth of July — normally a two and a half hour trip — take seven hours! This particular Sunday was not a holiday. We left a little later, hoping the brunt of the traffic had passed. As we approached the toll booth, we were pleasantly surprised, sailed through, and were elated. That elation turned to frustration immediately afterwards. Traffic had come to a complete stop! We had no idea why, but it was a bumper-to-bumper crawl almost all the way to the hotel. The trip took four hours. Considering the reason for this trip, our tensions were already elevated and the traffic only made it worse, especially for Brad. He hated these doctor appointments, especially having to travel to Boston for them.

We finally made it to the hotel, checked in, and then went downstairs to the hotel restaurant for dinner. We had no energy to head out into the city to explore. This was not a pleasure trip.

Garrett was landing at Logan by now. Brad had agreed to pick him up at the airport, but at this point he was fried and didn't have the energy to do so. Garrett graciously took a cab to the hotel. By the time Garrett arrived, Brad and I had already finished our dinner; Garrett hadn't eaten yet, so while Brad went back to their room, I waited for Garrett in the restaurant, so he wouldn't have to eat alone. It was 11 p.m. by the time I got to my room, and we would have to check out early to get to their 8:00 a.m. lab appointments at DFCI. Needless to say, Monday morning we were all tired and stressed. We were a little late for our appointment, which only added more stress, but eventually we made it.

Garrett's appointment took over two hours. Suneet could not make it, but his notes were included in the meeting. We talked about so much that it is impossible to reproduce it all here. We discussed Garrett's health status and the possibility of AML on the horizon. We were told that at that time, DFCI had completed two bone marrow transplants on DC patients in their 20s and neither had survived. We left with more questions than we had when we arrived.

After Garrett's appointment, Brad went in on his own with Eva and Lisa Brennan. Since we had already discussed bone marrow transplant, his appointment only lasted about an hour. When he was done, he came out and handed me his lab results from earlier that morning.

As we were waiting to wrap up, Eva and Lisa came to finalize things in the waiting room. Eva saw the ashen look on my face as I looked at Brad's CBC numbers. I discreetly pointed out three of Brad's CBC values that were of concern. She knew that I knew the reality of his numbers. She looked at me and nodded, and "mouthed" "I'll call you."

They said goodbye and headed back into the clinic. The three of us stood in the lobby waiting for the elevator when Brad looked at Garrett.

"How did your appointment go?" he asked somberly.

This moment broke my heart for our two sons. This wasn't two brothers asking "hey, how was your weekend," or "how's work going," or "how's your dating life going." It was "how did your rare genetic, highly fatal disease checkup go?" This was their reality, and it sucked!

As we left Boston, Garrett was very quiet, understandably so. We were both given so much clinical information our heads were spinning, especially his. Brad, though, seemed suddenly less tense. He actually said he was glad he had gone and told me he was going to have more follow through on his health care and asked for my help coordinating the many overdue follow up appointments that he needed. I don't know what happened in this particular appointment, but for the first time I felt like Brad was "owning" his illness, and had finally decided to do whatever necessary to take care of himself. The ride home was oddly much more pleasant, at least for Brad and me.

Brad dropped us off in South Portland, where Garrett and I got into my car and we stopped for lunch. During lunch I asked him how he was doing, since that had been a particularly intense appointment. He said he didn't want to talk about it. I respected that. We finished lunch in silence and headed to our hotel in Freeport, where we would be staying for three nights, so I could meet with contractors for the condo renovations and Garrett could meet up with friends before heading back to Florida on Friday.

Tuesday I was up early and headed straight to Brunswick. Garrett was wiped out and slept in with a Do Not Disturb sign on the room door. I checked in with him a few times throughout the day. By 5 p.m. he was ready to leave the room, so I headed back to the hotel. When I got to the room, I could tell he was upset, so I asked him if something was wrong.

"Yes," he said right away.

I asked him what he was upset about. He said he was angry.

"At who?"

"You," he said. "You and Dad, for what you did to me genetically."

I took a deep breath. I knew this had been coming and I understood. Why wouldn't a 27-year-old be angry for his unhealthy genetic DNA? It was logical to blame his parents. I told him that I understood.

"Garrett, you have to know that if Dad and I had any idea that we would have brought children into the world with a devastating genetic disease we would not have had children. How could a responsible adult do such a thing? I understand that you are angry at us and it's okay," I added.

Wednesday we did a variety of errands and were out and about most of the afternoon. While we were in Freeport, I used the car during the day and made sure Garrett could use it at night to see friends. Frankly, by the end of the day I just wanted to get back to the hotel, have a hot meal, and veg for the night. We were heading back to the hotel around 5 p.m. Garrett was in the passenger seat.

"I have to ask you a question," he said, staring straight ahead.

"Okay."

"If I die before my cat, will you promise to take care of her?"

I couldn't answer because I was choking back tears. We rode the rest of the way to the hotel in silence.

I dropped Garrett off Thursday morning in Portland, where he stayed with his best friend, Joey. He would spend the day and night at Joey's, then Uber to the airport first thing Friday morning and head back to Florida. (It's funny how "Uber" has become a verb in our vernacular.) I headed back to Sugarloaf, completely wiped out from watching the hell our sons had to go through every single day, knowing that it would never get better.

A Brief Respite

Wednesday, June 27, 2018. It has been six months since I last wrote. Wow. Yes, life gets in the way, but I know, deep down, that's not why I took a break from writing this book. I needed to take a break from the reality of Dyskeratosis Congenita. A lot has happened since I wrote, but I couldn't put it in writing. I still can't. When you look back and see the reality, which you are already keenly aware of, it takes on still another depth when it is right there, in black and white. It makes the reality harder, more painful somehow. I'm not sure when I will write again, but there's lots more to come...

It's Monday, July 30, 2018 now, and I'm at a little coffee shop in our new hometown of Brunswick, Maine. Brunswick has been somewhat of a respite from Dyskeratosis Congenita for our family. Each of us has really connected to our new community, welcomed it with arms wide open. There's something for everybody here and, even though our condo is small compared to any other place we've lived, we are all content. Having a place to feel at home is so important to anyone, but especially to a family that needs small comforts wherever it can find them. The comfort of our new surroundings is helping me get back to writing.

CHAPTER 15

More Ego and Condescension — "So, Mom is Here."

Early in November 2017 I headed back to Florida, sick with the flu and a broken bone in my foot. Garrett had an appointment with his hematologist. I didn't want him to be alone, since we were going to be discussing his most recent bone marrow aspiration results and the possibility that he had Acute Myeloid Leukemia. As I said earlier, we had not had a great experience with this doctor. Not only was today no different, it was actually worse.

Right away, the doctor was condescending. He greeted us with

"So, Mom is here. Mom hasn't been here for a while. How is Mom?"

I wasn't feeling well because I had a 101-degree fever, it was pouring rain outside, and I was trying not to slip with my corrective boot.

"Well, other than having a fever and a broken foot, I'm okay," I said, trying to be light about it.

"Okay, Mrs. Lincoln," he said.

If you don't know that reference— I certainly didn't — this was a quote from Mary Todd Lincoln after President Lincoln was assassinated, when she said "other than my husband being shot, I'm fine."

This was only the beginning of a horribly unprofessional visit.

He began by saying it was difficult for him to reach Eva at DFCI. My reaction was to offer him her cell phone number, and say that she had been amazingly wonderful to us by taking our calls. I also mentioned that one time she was in the operating room getting ready for a procedure, and still took our call.

"I thought she was a medical doctor, not a surgeon," he said.

Why couldn't he just accept the information I was giving him to help communicate about his patient? Plain and simple?

When we asked questions about Garrett's aspiration results, he said they were basically the same. We asked if there were any changes in the clonal cytogenetic abnormalities and he said no. If that was correct, we assumed this was good news; but he was vague and jumped around in what he was saying.

When we mentioned the correlation between the abnormalities and AML, he said that Garrett was not only in jeopardy of having AML, but all lymphatic cancers. We asked for clarification, but got none. This only added to Garrett's anxiety, and I told the doctor that.

"Yes, I know," he said. "He's called my staff six times for results."

Someone in his office had told Garrett the results were in, but could not be given out. We didn't understand.

He then went on a diatribe of questions that practically knocked us out of our seats.

"If you have three to five years left, is this how you want to spend your time?" he asked. "Do you have a therapist? Do you have a psychiatrist? What drugs have you tried for your anxiety? Are you religious, atheist, agnostic? Do you go to church? Or do you believe in God and just not go to church?"

At this point Garrett was so taken aback, he just said he was unsure. We did not understand the reason for these questions, nor were we sure they were even legal. The doctor went on to discuss issues about his own family members. What was wrong with this guy?

Twice I tried to interject or ask a question and he put his hand up in my face with his arm stiffly extended.

"Stop," he said. "Mom, you're trying to fix things."

He told me to be quiet and listen more. He told me I needed to be realistic and do more validating.

At this point, Garrett couldn't help but defend me and said that I wasn't "trying to fix things or not be realistic."

I tried to interject again to say that we were trying to help Garrett with his OCD and give him whatever positive possibilities were available. He didn't know Garrett on a personal level or live with him. Nor did he know the hell that Garrett — and all of us for that matter — have been through with his OCD, and all the hard work he does every day, especially in light of his diagnosis. I told him we were trying to give him tools when he's "on the ledge."

"Mom, stop. You're trying to fix things," he said again.

When I said we were all on the same team working on Garrett's behalf, he rolled his eyes and dismissed us.

It took me months to calm down from that one. Poor Garrett thought it was the fact that this doctor, who shall remain nameless, and I just didn't get along. Thankfully, and much to my surprise, our doctors in Boston helped Garrett to see things differently when we had an appointment at DFCI the following March.

Garrett's appointment at DFCI was intense, as always. Eva and Suneet began with a discussion of what had happened in November at the Florida clinic. They told Garrett that when a doctor puts his own ego ahead of his patient's care it is time to get a new doctor. They told him that what this doctor did was so wrong on so many levels, and it wasn't "Mom just being a mom." That acknowledgement meant more to me than I can express.

To jump ahead for a moment, Garrett moved back to Maine in December 2018. He has a whole new team of doctors yet again — and he never has to see that doctor again!

CHAPTER 16

Angst, Heartbreak, and Hope, 2018

From March to late August things with both Brad and Garrett were relatively calm, without any major additional appointments or health scares. We are always grateful for calm times.

In August, Nancy Cornelius, the cofounder of Dyskeratosis Congenita Outreach, whom I had met at that first Camp session, went to the University of Pittsburg Hospital, where she awaited a double lung and bone marrow transplant. We communicated via text and, as always, her sense of humor, along with her huge heart, prevailed. We texted several times during the week of August 19. On Friday night, I checked in with her to see how she was doing. She said she was going downhill a little every day. Her doctors were saying that they may have to intubate or trach her until she could get new lungs. I told her how much she was loved and what a pioneer she was for Dyskeratosis Congenita! I told her that, even though she wasn't "family," she personally had a huge impact on my family. She said she was going to sleep, but would try to be in touch soon. This haunted me.

I did not hear from her on Saturday August 25. By Sunday afternoon I was starting to freak out, so I texted her at 1:34 p.m. and just said "thinking of you." Bruce and I took a ride down to Harpswell to have lunch at a waterside restaurant. It was there I received a text from Rachel, a DC/Camp Sunshine family member, asking me if it was true that Nancy had passed on Saturday. I called the hospital immediately and learned the sad truth. I burst into tears. I thought she was going to beat this damn disease. She had to. She was our leader, who fought to the end. She was willing to put her body through any hell necessary if it meant the medical community could learn more about this awful disease. She didn't make it. There is another hole in my heart.

The biannual Camp Sunshine Dyskeratosis Congenita Retreat was approaching. It proved, as I expected, to be an intense retreat. They always are, but this one — without Nancy — was going to be brutal. It was.

At Camp, along with many seminars, meetings, and activities, there is also a balloon launch. The launch is an opportunity to send a loving wish to loved ones who have passed. To put things into perspective, 31 families from around the world attended Camp. Of those 31 families, 10 were "Legacy" families, which means that someone in their family had passed from Dyskeratosis Congenita. When you look at the small population of families affected with Dyskeratosis Congenita who attended, and the fact that one third of them were there because they had lost someone, it's pretty frightening.

The launch is a somber moment. At this particular launch, a 14-year old male DC patient from California, who is Scottish, played the bagpipes. All the balloons were white, with white strings attached.

Everyone took a marker and wrote a message to a loved one. Then we sang the Camp Sunshine song.

"Let's go stand in the back," Nancy's husband Skip said to me.

We stood there, arm in arm, with tears rolling down our checks. If you had known Nancy and Skip, you would know that their sense of humor complemented each other.

"Do you know what Nancy would say about this?" Skip said as the balloons were being released. "'It's like a hundred little sperm floating in the sky.'"

Picture a scene where it is so quiet you could hear pin drop, or someone's heartbeat, then you hear me break out into an enormous riot of laughter. Every single person at the launch turned around and looked at me. It was hysterically funny. It didn't feel like it exactly at that moment, but Nancy would have roared with laughter.

Skip's quote spread around camp, so much so that when Garrett and I returned to DFCI in December and I showed Suneet Skip's picture of the balloon launch — which was miraculous in its own right, since the balloons formed the shape of a butterfly — he said he had already heard about Skip's comment.

Camp is always intense, especially when you talk to other families in a matter-of-fact way about how their child died. It's hard going back to Camp not knowing who was able to return and who could not. I know of no other place like Camp. It embraces you, comforts you, and educates you, all under one roof. The bonds that are formed at Camp are unbreakable. When our family has something new on our proverbial plates because of Dyskeratosis Congenita, we reach out to our DC family, first and foremost.

During this particular Camp retreat, something amazing was shared with me that directly affects my family. I specifically wanted to speak to Suneet, since he is not only on the medical advisory board of Team Telomere, but is also part of our DFCI team. He knows Brad and Garrett personally. Since he had just seen Garrett recently, we were both feeling pretty good about Garrett's health status. However, Brad was overdue for lots of tests. I brought Brad's recent CBCs with me. I mentioned how his bruising had increased, as had his shortness of breath. I was concerned that his MCV values were increasing. There is a school of thought that as MCV value rises (MCV measures size of red blood cells), bone marrow failure gets worse. Suneet was concerned about Brad's numbers, and thought that he might be "shunting."

Since every time I go to Camp I learn something new, this was another unfamiliar term that I learned that day. To put it in lay terms, shunting means that the passageways that red blood cells move through enlarge. As they enlarge, it becomes more difficult for those cells to capture oxygen from the passageway walls, which means they travel through the heart and out to the rest of the body without enough oxygen. This is very dangerous for the entire body. I told Suneet I was concerned that if Brad's numbers continued to worsen, he might not be with us when I returned to Camp in 2020. Suneet only nodded.

Despite all this heavy, sad, serious stuff, Suneet said he needed to spend about 45 minutes or so with me, privately. He had something very important to share. Naturally, this piqued much more than just plain curiosity in me.

~

Dyskeratosis Congenita is a telomere biology disorder, first and foremost. Every living being, person, or animal, has telomeres. Telomeres are protective structures at the ends of chromosomes. As one ages, telomeres shorten. This is a natural part of the aging process. Picture a shoelace. It has protective caps at each end. These caps help keep the shoelace from fraying or shortening more quickly than it otherwise would. Patients with telomere biology disorders have shorter telomeres. This means that their chromosomes are not protected in a normal way, which is why they age more quickly and why they do not live as long.

~

On Saturday, Suneet and I finally found a window of time in-between sessions and went into the computer lab for privacy. He opened his laptop.

"Do you remember Brad signing up to be part of my study when he was diagnosed in December of 2011?" he began.

I said yes. He was so excited about what he was about to share. He explained that his team of researchers have been working diligently on this study and nothing else, and that from a scientific perspective, they had learned some major information in a very short time. One of the objectives of the study was to see if there is a way to lengthen telomeres in DC patients who have the PARN mutation! I believe Brad and Garrett are only two patients with a diagnosed PARN mutation out of a total of five in the world. This study couldn't just be about them! But it was!

Suneet explained as quickly as he could about how cells can go in different directions, good or bad. His team was trying to see what it would take to have the cells all go in a good direction by finding a way to lengthen telomeres. At this point my brain almost exploded! Could I really be hearing what I was hearing?

"Am I hearing you correctly? If you can find a way to lengthen telomeres, wouldn't every pharmaceutical company in the world want your information, since it could essentially reverse the aging process for every living being?" I asked.

"Well yes, but you're ahead of me," he said.

He explained they had discovered that if they add one particular molecule to a cell, they had evidence that telomeres were being lengthened in DC patients with the PARN mutation! My eyes could not believe what they were seeing! He showed me Patient Number 1's results. The added molecule made the telomere longer, not shorter, repeatedly. Then he showed me Patient Number 2's results. The telomere with the additional molecule was longer, not shorter, repeatedly. Patient Number 2 was Brad! Again, I couldn't believe it. There were a total of three patients in this study, which were all showing the same results in the lab. This was real progress! They were on the verge of being published. This was science at work, at its best!!

I asked him what lengthening telomeres would do for DC patients. He replied that the hope is to have a whole systemic effect, improving the quality of life for these patients. His passion for the work was flowing out of him. It seemed like he wanted to burst and tell everyone, but science takes time. They are working hard to get results for patients with just one mutation. Camp was not the place to share this information yet, because all the patients with the other 11 or 12 mutations would want to know who was working on theirs.

Suneet's work is far from over, and I feel positive that more beneficial information has yet to be discovered, but it is mind-blowing that our son is part of a process that is making medical history. He said that at a future point, they may need more samples from Brad and Garrett.

"Take all the samples you need," I said. "I know they're not my bodies, but please take what you need. Brad and Garrett may feel differently, but somehow, I don't think so."

In December, I asked Suneet if they were going to be doing a study comparing Brad and Garrett, since they are siblings with the same mutation who are manifesting the disease differently. He said yes, but again, I was getting ahead of it. Whether Brad and Garrett would benefit directly from this new medical information was yet to be seen. However, if they could help to prevent another living being from suffering from this horrible disease in any way, their contributions to science would be priceless.

YOU WON'T BELIEVE IT (BUT IT'S TRUE)

CHAPTER 17

November 29, 2018

At 6:15 a.m. my cellphone in Florida rang. I bolted out of bed to
see who would be calling so early. It was Garrett. He was at Mid
Coast Hospital in Brunswick. Brad had been vomiting blood. I
called Eva immediately. After many phone calls back and forth, we
decided I should fly back to Maine immediately, in case there was
another rupture. My head was spinning, both from the urgency of
Brad's health crisis and because I had only arrived in Florida 29 hours
earlier. Getting back to Maine was intense. On top of everything,
Brad was very angry that I was coming back. He must have been so
scared, and having me there would just make him more tense, but I
could not not be there. In my mind I kept hearing "if something
else ruptures you will want to be there."

I want to give a huge thank you to the Delta Airlines crew wherever
my connection was — I truly don't remember — into Portland. I
had asked a flight attendant if I could get off the plane first, so I could
get to the car rental place before it closed. The pilot made an
announcement asking all passengers to remain seated until I got off.
I made it to the car rental place then took the 40-minute drive to
our house. I couldn't understand why I couldn't see the road very well.
Cars were staying close to me and I didn't know why. As I approached
the final traffic light near our home, I came to a complete stop,

turned on my signal, and turned to go home when I was pulled over by a police officer. I started to shake and cry. What did I do wrong? By now it was 1 a.m. The police officer told me I didn't have my headlights on. I showed her my car lease agreement and told her why I was back in Maine. She asked me if my son was at Mid Coast Hospital. I said no, he had been transported to Maine Medical Center. She let me go without a ticket. I'd like to send her a huge thank you, also.

The whole time Brad was in the hospital he would not let me go in to see him. I respected his wishes, but it wasn't easy. Thankfully, Garrett and Brad's girlfriend Cyndee sent me regular updates. It turned out that Brad had had a portal hypertensive gastric hemorrhage because of his advanced liver fibrosis from his Dyskeratosis Congenita. He was put on meds and sent home on Saturday. When he came home to get some clothes, and while Cyndee was outside, he apologized for not letting me visit him, and thanked me for coming. I can only imagine how frightening it must have been for him.

He was being closely monitored by his gastroenterologist and things seemed to settle down. He came to Florida with me in mid-December and spent Christmas with us.

One evening while the two of us were out to dinner, he said there was something he wanted to tell me. He said he was taking "edibles" to help with the pain and to help him eat.

"Good for you Brad," I said immediately. "Do you know how many DC patients at Camp Sunshine take edibles or smoke pot to help with their pain? By all means, if there is something to give you relief, please take it."

I think he was surprised by my response. What he said next took me by surprise.

"Mom, if I'm still 'here' in 2020, I'd like to go to Camp with you."

Up until that point, he never wanted to go because he didn't want to see children younger and sicker than he was. What he said haunted me, though.

YOU WON'T BELIEVE IT (BUT IT'S TRUE)

CHAPTER 18

April 26, 2019 —
A Wait and See Situation

I was still in Florida with Bruce and it was still a normal day, or so I thought. Then Brad's gastroenterologist called to give us some dire news. Brad's liver fibrosis had turned to cirrhosis and at this point it was End Stage Liver Disease (ESLD). The only thing that could help Brad now was a liver transplant.

There is a score for the health of the liver from 1 to 40 — 1 is healthy; 40 is the absolute worst. The measurement is called MELD. Brad's MELD was 17. We were referred to Dr. Irun Bhan at Massachusetts General Hospital. Our appointment was May 21. We met with Dr. Bhan to discuss liver transplantation and then Brad went into the examining room. It would be at least a week to get results.

After Dr. Bhan received all the test results, he called to deliver the news. Due to Brad's bone marrow failure, Pulmonary Fibrosis, and ESLD put him at too high risk and he was not eligible for a transplant. *Boom.*

I could not accept that. I immediately contacted Dr. David Steensma, Brad's oncologist at DFCI and asked if they could reconsider accepting him as a liver transplant patient, if maybe there is something we missed.

Unfortunately, Dr. Steensma agreed with Dr. Bhan. However, he said if there was any chance of getting Brad to transplant, it would be by contacting the NIH, because they were making great strides in this area.

I immediately emailed Dr. Sharon Savage, who I knew from Team Telomere as one of our medical advisors. She responded immediately. She, too, understood the urgency. She strongly recommended that we contact the University of Pittsburgh Medical Center (UPMC). A referral letter is necessary to be considered for a transplant, and another doctor we had met in November 2014 immediately wrote a letter on Brad's behalf.

Now it was a wait and see situation.

CHAPTER 19

June, 2019

While we waited to hear from UPMC, we began working with the DKMS.org (an international nonprofit organization fighting against blood cancer and blood disorders) to organize a bone marrow drive for both Brad and Garrett, with the urgency being for Brad.

DKMS is an amazing organization and walked us through everything that needed to be done. On the day of the drive, wonderful friends helped out in ways we can't begin to thank enough. Huge kudos go out to the Yarmouth Fire Department, who showed up for a brother and allowed us to host the drive at the fire station. Chief Robitaille coordinated his crew to help us. Everyone was amazing. Brad, even though he was not feeling well, showed up. Garrett couldn't, and we understood. This event made their disease very public. Local newspapers and news stations did articles about them and their rare disease. It was very exposing.

I think it was good for Brad to come to the drive. He reconnected with his fellow firefighters. They embraced him. It was such a gift to watch that.

Unfortunately, most bone marrow drives do not help the person who needs a match, but they do expand the total bank of donors, which is priceless.

More than 100 people showed up. Many had to be turned away because of donor requirements. It was heartbreaking to say "thank you, but you can't be a donor." In the end our drive contributed 60 new donors to the bone marrow bank.

CHAPTER 20

University of Pittsburgh Medical Center

In early July we received the news that UPMC would accept Brad as a patient to be considered for the first-ever triple transplant: liver, bone marrow, and double lung.

Our appointment was for August 19. We flew to Pittsburgh on Sunday, August 18. Brad was already tense, but flying into Pittsburgh infuriated him. At the airport, images of all Pittsburgh's sports teams are displayed everywhere you look. Being a huge New England sports fan, Brad was disgusted.

The next three days were unbelievable. What Brad endured in those 72 hours made our trip the NIH in November 2014 seem like we had been at Disneyland.

We hit the bricks, so to speak, first thing Monday morning. Our first appointment was at 8 a.m. We didn't get back to the hotel until after 6 p.m., which was the only early day. The next few days were even more extreme. The myriad of appointments is too complicated and intense to detail.

One doctor we met with was very encouraging.

"We have never done three transplants on one patient," he told Brad. "You will be a human lab rat, but we feel we can help you."

Brad actually smiled. He got it. It was hopeful.

The critical appointment was meeting with the liver transplant doctor, Dr. Christopher Hughes. He was direct, yet calming. He discussed what this transplant meant in great detail, and felt that Brad would benefit greatly from it. However, while waiting for our next appointment, Karen Bailey, our transplant coordinator, came in to give Dr. Hughes an update on Brad's MELD. His MELD in April was 17, which on the scale from 1 to 40 wasn't good. It was now 30. The window of time to get Brad to transplant was closing. Brad left the room for a moment, Karen looked at me, and I burst into tears. I didn't want Brad to see me crying, but being the hyper-observant person that he was, he still caught me and asked if I was crying. I denied it. I couldn't bear to put any more stress on him.

While we waited to see the pulmonologist, we met a Camp Sunshine family member. He was also seeing the same doctor to seek a double lung transplant. It gives me great pleasure to say that this patient, husband, and father of three received his transplant and is doing well. Not many Dyskeratosis Congenita patients can say that.

Instead of what we thought was our call to see the pulmonary doctor, a nurse came out and said we had to cancel the appointment and rush Brad to the hospital. He was in severe need of a red blood cell and plasma transfusion. It was complicated. In the end they did not transport him via ambulance, but he was ushered immediately to the hospital. The transfusions had to be done at specific times. It was 9 p.m. before we got back to the hotel.

Brad said something to me during the transfusions that would become monumental in the near future. He could see the look of concern on my face. He knew that I knew the magnitude of what was happening. He wanted to prepare me for the future.

"Mom, *when* I go to transplant it's going to be a lot harder,' he said. "I need you to be stronger for me."

I "bucked up."

We returned to Maine that Thursday. We were both exhausted, mentally and physically.

It would be a few weeks before we would hear if Brad would be accepted as a transplant patient. A panel of almost 40 doctors review each patient's case, which is organized as a Power Point presentation. The patient's fate is in their hands.

Waiting to hear if Brad would be accepted was torture. Thankfully, he was. Now we had a huge road to travel. We had to find a liver for Brad. It was an unfathomable thing to understand. How do we go about asking anyone to offer part of their liver? A donor with a healthy liver can donate a portion of their liver to a patient and the donor's liver will grow back to almost 95% of its original size in about six weeks. The liver is the only organ that can rejuvenate itself. It is amazing what the human body can do.

CHAPTER 21

September, 2019

Brad was seeing his gastroenterologist regularly at this point.

He was very uncomfortable because he had lost a lot of weight, but his abdomen was quite distended from the accumulating ascites (fluids). A decision was made that he should have a paracentesis, a procedure in which fluids are drained from the abdominal cavity.

More than seventeen pounds of fluids were removed and Brad finally got some relief. He was able to stand erect and stretch, something he had not been able to do for quite some time.

YOU WON'T BELIEVE IT (BUT IT'S TRUE)

CHAPTER 22

October 7, 2019

At approximately 1 p.m. my cell phone rang. It was Cyndee. She was very concerned about Brad. He had a fever and had vomited. We spoke for a bit to try to figure out what we should do and decided that Brad should go to the hospital immediately. He was transported via ambulance to Maine Medical Center (MMC).

Bruce and I rushed to meet them at the hospital.

Brad was admitted, but had to wait for a room to open up. He was assigned to a temporary area while he waited. I stayed with him. MMC had contacted our team at UPMC to see if it was advisable to life flight him to Pittsburgh. His doctor was having a very hard conversation with Brad. He had to ask Brad whether, in the event things took a turn for the worse, he wanted to be put on life support. Who did he want to make decisions for his health in the event he was unable to do so for himself? I fought back tears. They decided that Brad was too sick to be flown to Pittsburgh, and that I would be his medical proxy.

Brad was finally admitted to his room, where he would only be for a few days before being transferred to a different floor. He was eventually transferred to the critical care floor.

Cyndee never left Brad's side except to shower. She slept in a chair every single night. Garrett and I took turns staying with them. We agreed that Bruce would take care of everything at home and be our runner if we needed anything, while still going to the hospital every day, as well.

Brad's health was deteriorating fast. Our team of five doctors and every nurse and technician were amazing. They were kind, compassionate, caring, and well skilled. Brad was in great hands and they were doing everything possible to get him through this infection, which they could not identify.

Brad endured more tests and procedures than I can recall.

Late afternoon on October 14 two of Brad's doctors asked to speak to me privately. I cry even now as I write this. They delivered the most difficult news — Brad's liver disease had spread to his kidneys and there was nothing else they could do. Even though I understood, I was not ready to accept this news. I asked his team of doctors to contact UPMC and talk with our team of doctors there to see if there was anything else that could be done. I said that if UPMC agreed with MMC, I would accept that conclusion.

On the morning of October 15, the doctors approached me in the hall to deliver the news that UPMC was in agreement with MMC. Now we had to tell Brad.

That morning Bruce had a 101-degree fever. He knew what we had to do and still wanted to come to the hospital so we could tell Brad together. But we realized he couldn't come to the critical care floor of the hospital. It would do Brad in, and possibly others.

We decided that the doctors and I would tell Brad that afternoon, with Bruce on speaker phone.

We had to tell Brad the awful news that there was nothing else that could be done for him. We had to give him the choice of staying in the hospital, going to a hospice house, or going into hospice at home in Brunswick. It was unbearable watching him trying to absorb this horrible information.

He had questions. One was whether he would be in pain.

"Brad if you decide to come home, there will be medication there so you will not be in pain. Also, if you come home, there will be no more bells (the bells in the hospital are intolerable), no more tests, and no more procedures," I said.

He looked directly at me.

"That's what I want," he said.

He chose to come home to Brunswick. Within an hour or so, an ambulance arrived. Brad adamantly stated that he did not want any pain medication because he wanted to be coherent for the ambulance ride. The irony that he was being brought home to die in an ambulance was a lot to bear, since he spent over nine years driving patients to the hospital, but it was important to him.

After we told him, he asked all of us to leave the room. I left and proceeded to lose it.

About 30 minutes later I knocked on the door and asked if I could come in.

"Yes, I particularly want to talk to you." he said. "Mom, I could hear Dad crying on the phone but you didn't, why was that?"

"Brad, do you remember when we were in Pittsburgh and you were getting your transfusions you said 'Mom, *when* I go to transplant it's going to be a lot harder. I need you to be stronger for me'? That's what I'm doing right now," I said.

He paused, thought, then said

"Thank you. I appreciate that."

Again, when I left his room, I broke down.

CHAPTER 23

Hospice

Even though both Brad and Garrett gave their consent for me to write this book, with the hope of maybe helping some other family, at this point I will no longer write about Brad's final days. I want them to be private for him, and our family. I do have to say that Cyndee stayed by Brad's side every single day, as did Bruce, Garrett, and I. Brad's friends came by often, along with many of our family friends. So many brought food, a shoulder to lean on, and lots of love.

The team of people from Chan's hospice were amazing and treated Brad with the utmost respect and care.

We lost Brad on November 8, 2019. He was only 33 years old. We miss him every single day. He was a warrior against a horrible disease that has taken too many.

YOU WON'T BELIEVE IT (BUT IT'S TRUE)

CHAPTER 24

Hope

Progress is being made on Dyskeratosis Congenita every single day. The bone marrow study that Brad participated in is making amazing headway. Brad is patient No. 2 of 3. Patient No. 2's DNA has contributed immensely to research, so much so that doctors from around the world are talking about Patient No. 2. As I mentioned earlier, Brad said that even though he may not live long enough to benefit from the research, he knew someone else might. Because of Brad's study participation, a new gene has been identified and it is helping to hopefully make possible a novel treatment for Telomere Biology Disorders. Brad's contribution may help his brother Garrett.

Brad did not let his disease define him. Brad's passion for life was best stated when he took a picture of Sugarloaf Mountain and posted on Instagram:

#Ichoosetoliveinadream

In Brad's memory, the "Choose to Live in a Dream" Brad Martin Memorial Golf Tournament has been established. We have applied for, and are awaiting, "Trademark" status for our logo so we can also sell merchandise to continue to raise money to support Brad's choice and Suneet's study. To learn more, kindly go to:

www.choosetoliveinadream.com

Also, even though Brad and Garrett are DC patients with the same mutation, Garrett is not manifesting Dyskeratosis Congenita the same way as Brad at all. He currently does not have bone marrow failure, pulmonary fibrosis, or liver fibrosis and, thankfully, is leading a very normal life. We continue to hope that science finds some of the many keys to this ever-evolving puzzle, and maybe even a cure for all DC patients.

EPILOGUE

This is a true account of our family's journey of the discovery about our two sons' diagnoses of a rare genetic disease.

It is meant to provide encouragement and tenacity to those in need during the most difficult of times. It is not intended to be any type of a medical guide or offer any medical advice. Its only objective is to let other families who may be going through a similar thing know that they are not alone.

Medical science is an amazing thing, even when the news is overwhelming. Science is always in the process of seeking better answers. Dedicated, passionate doctors and researchers continue the search for answers every single day.

ACKNOWLEDGEMENTS

An enormous thank you goes out to all of Brad's and Garrett's doctors. Each and every one of them is so dedicated to their patients and their families. They have all chosen a profession that has many difficult days. They often have to deliver unbelievably hard news to many people, yet they get up every day and continue to do their best to treat their patients.

Camp Sunshine — thank you for providing a beautiful lifeline for patients and their families to let them know they are not alone.

Team Telomere works hard every day to help find a cure for Dyskeratosis Congenita, a telomere biology disorder. You continue to provide the latest DC information. The support that is offered and the fundraising for research is priceless. Thank you for updating the only Clinical Guidelines available for this disease.

Karen Bailey, our transplant coordinator at UPMC. You were an amazing lifeline for us before, during, and after our trip to Pittsburgh. You fought like hell for Brad. Thank you so very much.

Jen Bradstreet, graphic designer, an enormous debt of gratitude goes out to you for offering to do the cover art for this book. You took my idea and hit it out of the park. You brought my vision of many years to life. You also so kindly offered to do the formatting of my book for print. Your generosity leaves me speechless.

Gail Clark, my dear friend. We have had many artistic and friendly journeys together. Your guidance to help me find a starting path to getting this book edited and published is appreciated beyond what my words can express.

Carole Fallon, who was so gracious and helpful to offer so many leads for editing and publishing options to someone who knew nothing about this industry.

Linda Lundborg of Tides Edge Design, who took the time to share editing options.

Lucie Teagarden, who took the time read this book and point me in the direction of an editor who would be a good fit for this book.

Suneet Agarwal, MD, PhD, who so kindly took the time to read this book and offer medical editing to be certain such valuable information was correct. Your words about my book mean more than I can say.

Tatiana Brailovskaya, my editor. Tatiana, thank you very much for your kind and gentle editing of my book. You always encouraged and protected my voice. You understood how important that was to me and you accomplished this task beautifully. I feel I have gained a new friend.

Last, but not least, a huge thank you goes out to all the people who have supported, and continue to support, our family throughout this ordeal. Your love and support does not go unnoticed or unappreciated.

REFERENCES

Eva Guinan, MD
Dana Farber Cancer Institute

Suneet Agarwal, MD
Dana Farber Cancer Institute

David Steensma, MD
Dana Farber Cancer Institute

Lisa Brennan, RN
Dana Farber Cancer Institute

Erik Larsen, MD
Maine Children's Cancer Center

Maine Medical Center
Portland, Maine

Blanch Alter, MD
National Institutes of Health

Sharon Savage, MD
National Institutes of Health

Christopher Hughes, MD
*University of Pittsburgh
Medical Center*

Karen Bailey, RN
*University of Pittsburgh
Medical Center*

Alex Vanni, MD
Lahey Clinic

Irun Bhan, MD
Massachusetts General Hospital

Jakob Tolar, MD
University of Minnesota

Brian McClune, MD
University of Minnesota

Andrew Dietz, MD
Los Angeles Children's Hospital

Brigham Women's Hospital
Boston, Massachusetts

Team Telomere
www.teamtelomere.org

Nancy Cincotta
Camp Sunshine

Yarmouth Fire Department
Yarmouth, Maine

Nancy & Skip Cornelius

DKMS Bone Marrow Registry
www.dkms.org

CHANS Home Health
& Hospice
Brunswick, Maine

SUPPORT

For more information about Dyskeratosis Congenita,
to download the Clinical Guidelines,
or to support Team Telomere, please go to:

www.teamtelomere.org

If you would like to support the ongoing Bone Marrow study,
contributions may be sent to:

Children's Medical Center Corporation
A Massachusetts Charitable Corporation
300 Longwood Avenue, Boston, MA 02115

Tax ID: 04-1174680

To Be Used for Dyskeratosis Congenita Research
in the Stem Cell Transplant Center Bone Marrow Study
of the PARN Mutation

If you would like to Support Camp Sunshine to help
families go to camp, contributions may be sent to:

Camp Sunshine
35 Acadia Road, Casco, ME 04015

If you are interested in becoming a bone marrow donor
or to organize a bone marrow drive, please go to:

www.dkms.org

ABOUT THE AUTHOR

Donna Martin is not an author and knows that
this is probably the only book she will ever write.
She was compelled to tell her family's story.
She resides in Maine and Florida.

The photos of Brad & Garrett on the
back jacket were taken by a professional
photographer on December 7, 2011.

Brad was diagnosed with DC on
December 8, 2011.

It was our last non DC day.

Made in the USA
Columbia, SC
08 February 2023

11372700R00076